Camping Activity Book for Families

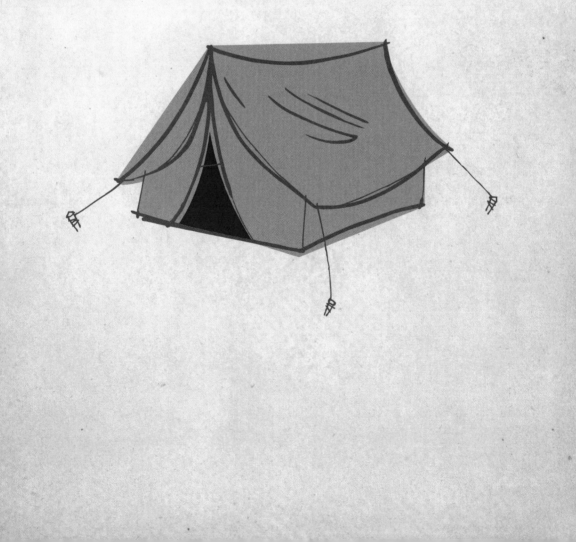

Camping Activity Book for Families

The Kid-Tested Guide to Fun in the Outdoors

Linda Parker Hamilton

FALCONGUIDES

GUILFORD, CONNECTICUT
HELENA, MONTANA

FALCONGUIDES®

An imprint of Rowman & Littlefield
Falcon and FalconGuides are registered trademarks and Make Adventure Your Story is a trademark of Rowman & Littlefield.

Distributed by NATIONAL BOOK NETWORK

Copyright © 2016 Linda Hamilton
Illustrations by Rachel Riordan © Rowman & Littlefield

All photos by the author unless otherwise noted

British Library Cataloguing-in-Publication Information Available

Library of Congress Cataloging-in-Publication Data Available

ISBN 978-1-4930-1334-0 (paperback)
ISBN 978-1-4930-1335-7 (e-book)

♾™ The paper used in this publication meets the minimum requirements of American National Standard for Information Sciences—Permanence of Paper for Printed Library Materials, ANSI/NISO Z39.48-1992.

CONTENTS

INTRODUCTION

All my best memories of childhood are outdoor adventures with my family, mostly day hikes among the pine and fir trees, granite boulders, mountain springs, and July wildflowers of the Eastern Sierras. On the trail to Thunder Mountain, where the Indian caves offered no fewer than five echoes reverberating off the rock face, we would stop for a snack in a meadow of lupine and mountain daisies. My mother would read aloud to us as we lay on our backs chewing grass and watching the floating, ever-changing menagerie of clouds in the blue sky. We sang songs in harmony as we walked. "Edelweiss," the "Country Marching Song," "Kookaburra," and "An Austrian Went Yodeling" were a few of the regulars. It was on a crimson mountain evening my dad taught me to play cribbage, and on another when I finally triumphed over him. On Silver Lake I learned to skip rocks, to turn my small hands into a water pistol, to fish, to paddle a canoe, to catch a crawdad, and once I created a ladybug hospital out of the tackle box when the surface of the water was covered with them.

Back home my parents had their routines, their weekend tennis matches. My brother and I had our homework and baseball practices. At home the television came on in the evening, and all conversation ended. In the mountains we talked.

> *These things are fun and fun is good.*
> —Dr. Seuss

I learned about my parents' childhoods. We laughed together. We did activities

together. We shared lazy afternoons reclining with hors d'oeuvres and watching aspen leaves dance and the sun shimmer on the lake.

Now that I'm a parent myself, I try to regularly set aside time away from our hectic schedule to create moments like these and take my kids out into nature. Camping can be a great time for family. In the outdoors you have the opportunity to be with one another in a meaningful way that can be hard to re-create at home in the every-day land of work and obligations, electronic entertainment, and society. While camping or even staying in a rustic cabin, you can be active and present: hiking, biking, fishing, swimming, and exploring the environment in all kinds of ways. You can relax in a hammock or camp chair, listen to the world around you, and let your thoughts wander. You can breathe fresh air and engage in life in its basics: Prepare food simply, set up your own home away from home, and feel a sense of belonging with nature and the people around you. This is the stuff of treasured, lifelong memories.

But sometimes it can be a struggle to engage the kids in experiencing the world around them. Sometimes we find ourselves tangled in tent poles wondering how to have the kids help but not get in the way. Sometimes we want to reconnect our busy family, but it just isn't happening. Sometimes we have a reluctant camper. And sometimes we just want to add a little more fun.

The *Camping Activity Book for Families: The Kid-Tested Guide to Fun in the Outdoors* will help you do all these things and have a darn good time doing it. The goal is to help families get the most out of camping and being in the outdoors, to have fun and discover new things about nature and one another while creating cherished memories. Camping trips are going to get better than ever!

The best part? A lot of the activities in here don't have to be done just while camping, so even when you're home you can continue the fun and sharing and make more memories!

HOW TO USE THIS BOOK

This book is designed to be a handy guide to making your family camping experience extra fun. Read this at home before you leave, and bring it with you to use during your trip. Choose activities that appeal to you. Have family members choose something that appeals to them. You might ask older kids to take charge of certain activities (for example, leading a game to keep everyone occupied while you're making lunch, or even helping to make lunch for everyone). Put younger children in charge of picking one family activity for each day or collecting the rocks and sticks needed for an activity. Follow the easy-to-read instructions, or let the games and crafts spark your own creativity.

The first couple of chapters provide advice on planning your trip—preparing, packing, getting the kids excited, and setting everything up for a successful outing with the family. Chapter three focuses on the most popular family outdoor pastime that will likely be your main activity each day, from hiking

> *There is something of the marvelous in all things of nature.*
>
> —Aristotle, ancient Greek philosopher

to birding to fishing. This isn't a how-to guide for each activity, but you'll find ideas for making sure each planned activity is as successful and family-friendly as it can be. After that you'll find tons of ideas on how to keep everyone

Photo by Kevin Meynell

engaged during the natural ups and downs of the day, with chapters on ways to explore and be active in nature, games you can play outdoors, outback arts and crafts projects, and favorite camp songs to sing. You can find quiet-time activities, energy busters, solo activities, and recommended ages for fun and games of all kinds in the Activity Finder at the end of the book. Of course, each child and family is unique, so use this as a general guide. You know your kids best.

Enhancing each chapter are sidebars with fascinating facts that will bring you even closer to nature ("Did You Know?"), special tips for kids ("Psst . . . Kids!"), topics for conversation ("Family Conversation Starters"), and jokes to share ("Laugh Time!").

Many activities include suggestions for recording the experience in a NATURE JOURNAL.

This is highly recommended but really depends on whether individual campers are into it or not. There are also options for being a PHOTOJOURNALIST. A camera is one of the few pieces of technology we recommend you bring along. (See chapter 1 for more information on Nature Journals and being a Photojournalist.)

the cottage

AT HOME BEFORE YOU GO

Everyone in the family can help in the research and preparation of your camping trip, and it gives them more ownership of the experience. Even the anticipation can be fun! If you have new or very young campers, introducing them to some of the equipment and aspects of the camping experience can inspire comfort and confidence. A little familiarity can go a long way.

> *Adopt the pace of nature: her secret is patience.*
>
> —Ralph Waldo Emerson

Picking a Campground

As long as you are well prepared and supplied, you can stay anywhere. However, for younger or inexperienced campers, it's a good idea to stay at a **developed campground,** one with flush toilets and hot showers and fully equipped sites with a picnic table, fire pit, and bear box. If some family members just won't camp, look to rent a rustic or developed cabin or tent cabin. Many state and national parks and private campgrounds have limited numbers of these. If you've gone camping before and are interested in roughing it a little more, consider walk-in campsites, rustic camping like on Bureau of Land Management (BLM) land or national forest land, where you have to bring everything in, or backpacking. Occasionally you can find backpack destinations with pack animals, llamas or donkeys, available for hire to carry your gear. This can be a worthwhile expense when camping with very small children, who often require additional gear.

Think about the distance from home and how many days you have to camp. Want to start simple and just do one overnight? You might be able to find someplace close to home that still feels like a world away. Less driving, more camping!

Think about what amenities/camping activities are most important to the family, and narrow down your choices accordingly. What do you want to do on your camping trip? Hike? Swim? Ride bikes? Take in nature programs and community campfires with a ranger? Climb rocks? Have privacy? Also consider what activities might be available nearby. There's so much fun to be had in nature, but if the kids are less than enthusiastic about getting away from it all, consider an area where you can take a trip to an off-site attraction that will entertain them.

Photo by Kevin Meynell

Research the campground conditions and environment. Is there poison oak? Is there a lake or river nearby? Have there been any bear sightings recently? Be prepared, and go with your comfort level. If you're planning way ahead, don't forget to check weather conditions for the appropriate season. Check out online reviews to understand the kind of crowd to expect, seasonal differences, and input on the best campsites.

> **Did You Know?**
> Poison oak does not grow above 5,000 feet elevation. Western poison ivy, however, grows at 8,500 feet in New Mexico and Colorado.

Know the amenities, and pack accordingly. Does the camp host sell firewood? Are there flush or pit toilets? If pit, bring more toilet paper! Do you need to bring your own grill? Are the sites shaded, or should you bring a tarp or canopy?

Plan to arrive during daylight hours. It's much easier to set up. You can see what you're doing. It's especially important for inexperienced campers or for anyone a little nervous about nature. The best part is being able to look around, get your bearings, and start exploring and playing in nature right away, as well as have your first meal in the campground.

Technology in Nature

Decide on technology usage rules before you leave home. If you want no phones or other devices, be clear about why. Make your reasons positive: "We're going to experience new things and places, the things you sometimes see on your iPad. This is going to be an adventure,

WHY ENCOURAGE YOUR CHILD TO BE THE FAMILY PHOTOJOURNALIST?

Photojournalism builds many skills. Along with keen observation, kids learn how to approach a live subject quietly to catch it in action. This builds patience and alertness. Kids become more aware of their surroundings, and this generally leads to increased curiosity and motivation to learn about what they see and experience. Photojournalists try to capture moments of truth, have compassion for their subjects, and take pictures that tell stories. Kids learn the basics of photography too: different types of shots, angles, and lighting.

From age 2 or 3 all through adolescence, children are developing their memory. The human mind tends to be very visual and remembers things that stand out. Competing with the colorful palette or photorealism of video games, it helps to make a record of your adventure in nature—whether a slideshow, book, or album—so it can be remembered with affection. Your children will be more likely to want to repeat such experiences.

and focusing on it makes it all the better." If you decide on limited usage, explain the rules. Though a hiatus from video games and habitual texting—for both kids and adults—while camping and limited use of technology in general is best, some technology can be put to great use in the outdoors.

It is empowering for kids (and shutterbug parents) to take pictures to memorialize their camping trip and to fine-tune powers of observation. There are suggestions throughout this book for your young PHOTOJOURNALIST. After the trip, your kids and you can turn the pictures into a slideshow or photo

book, which continues the fun and benefits the entire family, solidifying memories and encouraging campers to reflect on their experiences.

Kids love to share things they see and to connect with their friends, so you could have one time a day when they send pictures via Instagram or text message to relatives and friends. Or wait until you're in the car heading home for outside communication.

A great use of your smartphone while camping is for apps like geocaching or star and planet finders. If you don't have field guides for the flora and fauna in your area, a smartphone—with reception—can be useful as a walking encyclopedia. You can also listen to a camp song on YouTube to teach to the family.

The rules of technology use are up to you, but you have to follow them too. You can adjust them if what you initially decided doesn't work, but once you set them, don't break them!

Think Like a Child

Once the adventure begins, don't push the pace. Be aware of your own agenda. If you camped PK (pre-kid), plan on doing different stuff, doing less, going slower, and covering less distance. Bring patience to camp, and pay attention to how children and any new campers respond to activities, suggestions, and the new environment. Let kids find their own pace and choose some of the activities. They might need encouragement to try new things; but to make camping a positive experience,

it's important not to push kids into situations they find scary. And it might surprise you what they find scary.

Provide chill time. Longer vacations have waves of emotions. After the first exciting day or two, there is almost always a day or a few hours when energy dips and moods swing. Small children can suddenly get very upset by little things. Older kids can get sullen or homesick. Adults can get cranky and short-tempered. Make sure your children know that if they feel this way, they should tell you. Make sure they know it's totally normal. Give them (and yourself) a chance to RECHARGE. You don't have to do or see everything on the agenda.

Read aloud to your children, or do a quiet one-on-one activity or paper-and-pencil game (see page 150). If the family is in the middle of an excursion and can't be back in camp when a down period is needed, find other ways to take a break.

Psst...Kids! Everyone needs to RECHARGE at times. If you are feeling annoyed by a family member, tired of the sun, and ready to go home, take some time and be nice to yourself. Rest, nap, relax, read, doodle, or just get out of the sun or wind. Ask yourself what would recharge you? Play a game of cards. Lie on your sleeping bag and breathe for a while, or sit and watch the trees blowing in the breeze. Daydream and let your mind wander. Some people even like to have a good cry. After a recharge, you can usually once again enjoy your family and the great outdoors.

It could be something simple, like having a cool sip of water or splashing water on their faces. Have them throw a towel over their heads or put on sunglasses to block out some of the stimuli.

Don't overschedule. Not every activity needs to be carefully planned. If kids get into imaginary play, for example, maybe the swim or hike you had in mind can wait ten minutes. The kids might find a decomposing stump to take apart, or they might take more time with an activity than you expected. Give them time and space to play and explore, supervising as appropriate for their ages.

Outdoor & Camping Ethics

Model the behavior you expect of your children, and be clear about your expectations. Bring extra trash bags and keep a clean camp, be considerate of other campers, stay on trails, tread lightly around wildlife. Give your children opportunities to be responsible too. It will build their confidence and give you all a unified purpose. Your children are the next stewards of our Earth.

Decide on your family's ethics concerning the natural environment. The general rule of camping is to "Leave No Trace." None of the games in this book leave trash in the wild. In fact, you will find ways to make games out of cleaning up the forest! None of the games disturb living things (with the exception of bug, lizard, and crawdad hunting, which involves the

temporary displacement of these animals). A number of the games do involve moving and using rocks and sticks and other debris. You decide, depending on where you camp and your beliefs, whether to put the natural debris back as close as possible to where you found it or to leave your rock sculptures and leaf creations for other campers and hikers to discover and enjoy.

Always practice safety first. When doing activities involving being on the ground or picking up leaves and sticks, for example, know how to identify poison oak and poison ivy. When picking up bugs and critters, don't pick up anything with your bare hands that you don't know to be safe. Supervise your children in the camping kitchen, around the fire, and using tools, especially if they are inexperienced. Decide how far away and where kids can go on their own based on their age and your own comfort level. Boundaries make kids feel safe (parents too) and are even more important in new surroundings. In any activity, make sure you have the right age-appropriate safety equipment for everyone.

Family Camping Checklist

Here's a basic checklist to help make packing easier and to get everyone accustomed to camping supplies. Personalize this for your family, adding your own essentials. What may be an "extra item" for one family might be a necessity for another. The items on this list are for car or walk-in camping. Backpackers would probably want to trim this list down even more. Make sure your car is in good working order before departing.

Information/Personal Stuff

- ❑ ID, reservation info, address and directions, money (wallet)
- ❑ Cell phone and charger
- ❑ Camera and batteries

Sleeping/Bedtime

- ❑ Tent and tent footprint or tarp
- ❑ Sleeping pads
- ❑ Sleeping bags and/or sheets and blankets
- ❑ Pillows
- ❑ Books
- ❑ Comfort items like stuffed animals or blankies (optional)
- ❑ Extra blanket(s) (optional)

Light & Fire

- ❑ Lantern
- ❑ Headlamps and flashlights with extra batteries (1 light per person and at least a couple extra)
- ❑ Matches, a disposable lighter, or a butane stove lighter
- ❑ Fire starters or newspaper

First-Aid Supplies

- ❑ Bug repellent
- ❑ Sunscreen
- ❑ Acetaminophen or ibuprofen (or aspirin) for kids and adults
- ❑ Calamine lotion
- ❑ Tecnu or bentonite clay or other poison oak and ivy rash preventer

- ❏ First-aid kit with adhesive bandages of different sizes, tweezers, antibiotic cream
- ❏ Any prescription meds

Toiletries

- ❏ Toothbrushes, toothpaste, floss
- ❏ Soap
- ❏ Deodorant
- ❏ Hairbrush & hair bands
- ❏ Lip balm
- ❏ Feminine hygiene products—tampons & pads
- ❏ Toilet paper
- ❏ Towels (1 large and 1 hand towel for each camper)
- ❏ Moisturizing lotion or aloe vera

Clothing

- ❏ An outfit to play in for each day plus 1 or even 2 extra (Think mud and wet.)
- ❏ Long pants or tights and long-sleeve shirts, sweaters, or sweatshirts for morning and evening (possibly long johns)
- ❏ Jackets (Consider bringing 1 light and 1 winter/year-round jacket.)
- ❏ Warm hat
- ❏ Hat with sun visor, such as a baseball cap
- ❏ Extra socks (Long socks protect against ticks and poison oak/ivy.)
- ❏ Sunglasses
- ❏ Bathing suits (and goggles)

- ❏ Rain jackets, ponchos, or garbage bags
- ❏ Pajamas
- ❏ Flip-flops, sandals, or water shoes (for water play, showers, and middle-of-the-night bathroom runs)

Kitchen/Campsite

- ❏ An extra tarp (to hang for rain cover or general use)
- ❏ 2 or more ropes (for hanging tarp, for hanging clothes to dry, and more)
- ❏ Camp chairs
- ❏ Medium pot with lid, skillet, and mixing/salad bowl
- ❏ Knife & cutting board
- ❏ Cooking utensils: spatula, wooden spoon, tongs
- ❏ Pocketknife (extra knife, can opener, bottle opener, corkscrew)

- Plates, bowls, silverware, mugs, cups
- Plastic tub for washing dishes, sponge, dish soap
- Paper towels and wet wipes
- Garbage bags
- Zipper-lock plastic bags (large and sandwich size) for leftovers and easy away-from-camp lunch and snack packing
- Water—water bottles for each camper/hiker and 2 jugs or 1 5-gallon and one smaller (Refill at campground. Most have potable water; do your research. Bring more than you think you'll need for rustic camping.)
- Duct tape (for activities and crafts as well as repairs)
- String or twine (also used for crafts and activities as well as necessities)
- A folding backpacking shovel (for when nature calls away from camp and for activities)
- For walk-in camping, a kids' wagon to tote supplies to the campsite. (You won't regret it!)

Entertainment Necessities

- Deck(s) of cards
- 5 or 6 dice (6 for Farkle; 5 for Yahtzee, Skunk, and other games)
- A couple permanent markers
- Paper and pen and pencils (with sharpener)
- Nature journal (See page 14 for preparing a NATURE JOURNAL.)
- Camera (See page 3 about being a Family PHOTOJOURNALIST.)
- Additional items as required (May be required for specific games and activities listed in this book, though most make use of found objects or camp supplies that you'd readily have at hand.)

Photo by Kevin Meynell

Special Extras

Adding a couple special items can add some really fun times at the campsite. Bring them out as a nice surprise or when enthusiasm is dwindling and you need a little *shazam!*

Photo by Kevin Meynell

Consider bringing field guides, star charts, compasses, a magnifying glass, binoculars, or books to read aloud to the whole family. Bring musical instruments, percussion instruments, and songbooks. Some sporting equipment can be fun to use together around camp or to entertain the kids while parents are taking a breather. Tennis balls can be used in many different ways. Perhaps your family would prefer a Frisbee, soccer ball, horseshoes, or a hula hoop.

You don't need many arts and crafts supplies to make some great nature art, but if you are a particularly creative bunch, you could bring paint (acrylic for rocks), solar-print paper, fabric paint and T-shirts, colored yarn, or lanyard supplies. Bubble liquid and wands pack light. Walkie-talkies can be both fun and practical. Take the scary out of the night with glow sticks and a fiber-optic lamp for the picnic table. Try looking through your old toy bins for more entertainment options. Ignored toys and games often take on a new life in new surroundings.

Food, Glorious Food

Food in the outdoors just tastes better. With a little extra preparation at home, you can minimize your cooking time, leaving more time for fun. Once in camp, involve kids in food preparation, setting the picnic table, and washing dishes. You're all in this together and can take more time than during those rushed mornings before school or 20 minutes to get dinner on the table between piano lessons and soccer practice. Make food prep at home and in the campground a family activity.

Psst . . . Kids! Helping your parents plan, shop for, and prepare meals before your trip is a good way to make sure you get food you like!

Photo by David Rolf

and being able to use the containers for other activities. Salads that travel well, like bean, pasta, and potato salads, taste even better after several days. You can also pre-cook your favorite rice, noodle, quinoa, and polenta side dishes at home. Plain cooked rice and noodles are easy to reheat as well. You can even pre-fry bacon and sausage and quickly refry it at camp. This eliminates the need to discard bacon grease.

Freeze foods. Marinate or spice and freeze meat. Freeze the butter. With a little defrosting it will be ready to go—and it will help keep the cooler cold. Double-bag cheese and meats or anything else that can be ruined by melting ice in the cooler. You can also pre-make pancake batter and freeze it. Put it in a gallon-size plastic bag and just cut off the tip in camp to pour the batter in the skillet. This eliminates the need to wash a mixing bowl and spoon. You can also repurpose a ketchup bottle or glass jar for "shake and pour" pancakes. Do you like your pancake with fruit? Freeze some berries, banana slices, or mango chunks for the purpose. Freeze bottles filled with water. They will be nice and cold for your first day of hiking and help keep food fresh.

Plan the meals. Before you leave, write down all the meals, including snacks, you will need for your camping trip (Day 1: lunch, snack, dinner, dessert; Day 2: break-fast, trail snack, lunch; and so on), and make a menu plan for each, simple or elaborate. Use this list to create your pack-ing/grocery list. Remember to include condiments (ketchup, mustard, barbecue sauce, and the like). Recruit the kids, and let them choose some of the snacks or meals.

Pre-make what you can. Stew, soups, casseroles, spaghetti in sauce, and slow cooker meals can all be made at home and brought to camp in plastic containers. An added benefit is easy storage of leftovers

Psst . . . Kids! Make your pancakes a little more fun. Pour your batter on the skillet to make one big round pancake and two small ones attached to the big one at the top. On your plate, add fruit or nuts to make eyes and a nose and finish your bear cake! What other shapes can you make?

Wash and package healthy snacks. Wash and cut up fruit and vegetables before leaving, and put them into sealed plastic bags or small storage containers. It makes it easy to get these healthy snacks out quickly. This is also true of vegetables you wish to steam for dinner.

Organize your cooler. Label containers with tape and markers, giving all campers the ability to find things in the cooler and help out more in the camping kitchen. (Kids can help with the labeling.) Make sure the most-used items or first few meals are packed near the top for easy access and so the cooler stays open for less time. Buy ice as close to the campsite as possible, and divide it up into ziplock plastic bags to avoid flooding food and allowing you to distribute it as needed in the cooler. Keep your cooler in the shade by day, and reorganize it on occasion if things get shuffled around. A good cooler makes a great extra seat too.

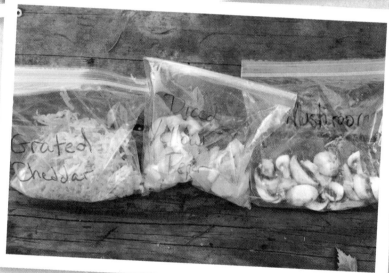

Use less commercial packaging. Prepackaging only what you need and taking items out of commercial packaging before your trip means less garbage at camp and fewer pieces in the packing puzzle. Save money and space by packing your own small containers of condiments. Empty beaten eggs into a mason jar for easy travel, and pour them out to make scrambled eggs or omelets. (Make personalized omelets by pouring egg into ziplock bags along with desired ingredients, seal the bags well, and boil them in water in a pot on your cooking stove.) Hard-boil some eggs, and cut your egg carton in half to carry them compactly.

Have the first campground meal ready and handy in your cooler so you don't have to stop setting up camp to make a meal and can take it easy after the drive in. Sandwiches are great; so is a precooked entree. Add drinks, veggies, and fruit and you've got a meal.

Make campfire meals fun. Cooking meals over a campfire can be exciting and empowering for kids. You can find great recipes for aluminum foil packet meals in cookbooks or online (try allrecipes.com or

usscouts.org). Most can be prepped at home, and you can cook the foil packets on a grill over an open fire or in embers. You can even cook scrambled eggs in paper bags over a grill. These websites also have recipes for Dutch oven cooking. You can roast hot dogs and meatballs, rolls and toast, pigs in a blanket, shish-kebobs, marshmallows, and

Photo by Kevin Meynell

more on sticks or skewers (check out reserve america.com/outdoors/skewer -recipes-for-campfire-meals .htm). Pie irons can also be used to cook entrees and desserts over the fire. Check them out at pieiron.com/recipes.htm.

Bring a few fun kitchen extras. For some added variety in food preparation or consumption, bring straws or silly straws, try out a solar oven (prepurchased or made; look for instructions and recipes online), or bring a battery-operated blender for smoothies or a container to make sun tea.

Try repurposing. Like the pancake dispenser, there are many other clever ways to repurpose food packaging and the like:

- *Reading lamp.* Wash a gallon milk jug and fill it with drinking water. At night, point a headlamp into the water to make a nice light on the picnic table or in the tent. You can drink from it *and* read by it!

- *Fire starters.* Wad up dryer lint and stick it inside a toilet paper tube for an effective campfire starter.

Photo by Kevin Meynell

- *Toilet paper caddy.* Put a roll of TP in an old coffee can or oatmeal container with lid to keep it dry and ready for use in any weather. Fashion a handle out of duct tape. Tape a ziplock plastic bag on the side and fill it with other baggies so they are handy to pack out paper from nature poops. Tape another ziplock bag on the side to hold sanitizer or hand soap. It's your nature poop caddy!

- *Travel spices.* Use labeled Tic Tac containers for spices. The Tic Tacs can be kept in a baggy and used as trail treats or edible game pieces.

- *Individual coffee bags.* Fill a filter with enough of your favorite coffee grounds for one cup. Tie with thread, baker's twine, or a twist tie at the top so it is securely closed. Make enough of these for your trip, and freeze them in a gallon bag to store in your cooler. When it's time for coffee in camp, just drop one in a mug of hot water and let it seep for several minutes for great instant coffee.

- *Kitchen organizer.* A hanging pocket shoe organizer hung on a tree branch or secure clothesline can hold nonfood items for your kitchen as well as first-aid supplies, sunscreen, playing cards, and more. The kind with clear pockets means less labeling. You can also repurpose a tool organizer for your camping kitchen. Need a place to put your cooking vessels? Wrap a leather belt around a tree, and use hooks to hang pots and pans.

Making Food Bear Safe

Though it's great to see critters in nature, you don't want to attract them to your camping kitchen. A bear in camp could create a traumatic moment for the family, and it's not healthy for chipmunks and birds to eat human food. Use any metal food lockers provided for coolers as well as food. Parks near bear habitats often require that you use bear-resistant canisters for food storage, so do your research. Keep your tents and sleeping area as far as you can from your kitchen. Don't leave your food unattended while you're away from camp. Food never belongs in the tent, even in the rain. Check children's backpacks and jacket pockets for forgotten snacks before bringing them in. Dispose of your trash in the bear-proof trash cans provided, or else burn what you can and double-bag the rest to pack out. And be sure to leave your campsite clean for the next campers. This includes picking up those random pieces of cereal and fruit pits that may have found their way to the ground.

Nature Journals

Nature journals are a great way to get in touch with your surroundings and capture and remember all you see and experience, creating a lasting log of your trip. Our family considers a nature journal a necessity, because there are so many ways to use it while camping, even if you just tear out the paper to make paper airplanes or to play paper-and-pencil games. Many of the suggested games and activities in this book contain a NATURE JOURNAL component.

Campers can each have their own personal journal, or you can just have one communal journal for the whole family to share and write in.

At its most basic, a nature journal could be as simple as a store-bought composition notebook or spiral binder, which you can add onto and customize as fits your needs. Or you can make your own from scratch, allowing campers to make theirs unique and personal to them.

Psst ... Kids! Your nature journal doesn't have to be "perfect." It is okay if it has crossed-out words, sentence fragments, unfinished drawings, and stick figures. Trying to make your journal perfect might hold you back from using it. Journals give you an opportunity to let your thoughts flow naturally while you lose yourself in your subject, whatever it is. The pages of your journal may look nothing like someone else's journal, and that's okay too. One person might like to write facts about all the cool stuff she sees. Another might like to make up stories or describe what he sees or how he feels when looking at a beautiful view. Someone else might prefer to color and draw, inspired by nature. A journal is also handy to use for pencil-and-paper games, to make stuff, or to tally how many cool animals or insects you see on your hike. Let your journal be a reflection of YOU!

Ideally you want a securely bound pad (glued, tied, or spiral bound) without lines so you can create your own compositions on each page and to allow for writing, drawing, and collecting fallen leaves, photos, and cutouts. It should be small enough to fit in a day pack, have a sturdy cover, and stay open when you're working on a page.

To make your journal extra usable and special, tie a push pen or mechanical pencil to it with string or make a *plastic pencil pouch* (say that ten times fast!) by taping a ziplock bag to the front. This pouch can also be used to hold colored pencils, a magnifying glass, and tape and to

The Juice on Journals

Scientists and researchers commonly keep nature or field journals as an important part of their work—recording their observations, hypotheses, and findings, as well as daily and seasonal changes and their effects on plants and animals. If naturalist and scientist Charles Darwin hadn't kept a nature journal on his famous voyage of the *Beagle*, we might not have known about all his amazing discoveries, thoughts, and theories. His journals are priceless artifacts today. Darwin once said about making notes in the field: "Trust nothing to the memory, for the memory becomes a fickle guardian when one interesting object is succeeded by another still more interesting."

collect small trail treasures. If desired, add another cool feature by creating an over-the-shoulder strap for your journal out of string or duct tape. Your children can hike or explore with their journals accessible and ready for use. Have children write their name on the inside or outside cover with a message to please return the journal if found, along with a parent's e-mail address and/or home phone number.

First entry. Suggest to kids that they make their first entry before leaving home. They can write about where the family is going camping and print and cut out pictures to paste in. They may want to add what they would like to see or do or how they are feeling about the trip.

Preparing New Campers

You can play games at home before going on your adventure in nature to get used to all the camping gear and learn more about being in the outdoors and what to expect. It's a really fun way to get ready!

Name That Camping Thing! *(ages 2 and up)*

See if you can identify this object you take with you when camping . . . blindfolded!

Supplies: Camping supplies, bandanas or blindfolds of some kind (optional)

1. Players sit in a line or circle with eyes closed or with blindfolds on.
2. The leader hands one common camping and hiking supply or tool to one player, who feels it and hands it to the next player, and so on.
3. Players guess aloud what it is and what it is used for. Repeat with a new object.

Variation

If the players don't know what the object is, they can call out "Creative!" and make up something wild about the object. A clever reply can earn a point.

Laugh Time!
Q: How do you convert a purse into a sleeping bag?
A: Put it to sleep.

Backyard Camping *(ages 3 and up)*

Get to know your tent at home before going camping. It'll transform your back yard! This also works as a good trial run for families who have never camped before.

Supplies: Tent, sleeping bags or sheets and blankets, pillows

1. Set up your tent in the back yard.
2. Play in it as a fort during the day:
   - Read a book in it.
   - Bring your stuffed animals or dolls in it.
   - Play with a soft ball in it.
   - Play a board game in it.
3. At night, have a family campout in the back yard and spend the night in the tent with at least one parent. In the morning, talk about the experience.

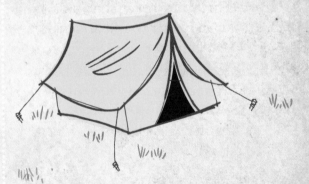

Nocturnal Exploration *(ages 4 and up)*

Get to know the night!

Supplies: Warm jacket, flashlight or headlamp (or both), short book (optional)

Stay up a little late and do something exciting and new right at home. Go into the back yard or someplace outside close to home after dark. Be sure to bundle up! Give your eyes

3. Experiment using a flashlight and shining it around you.

4. Sit somewhere comfortable and read a storybook by headlamp. (For younger campers, you can do this inside with the lights off.)

time to adjust, and look around. Use your various senses. Talk about what you experience. The idea is to become more acquainted with the night. Acquaintance is one of the best ways to rid ourselves of fear. Consider doing this a few times to get more comfortable with nighttime sounds and shadows. For younger children, make the night visits brief.

1. Look up at the night sky. Do you see stars and planets? Airplanes? Satellites? If you live in the suburbs or the city, you won't believe how many more stars you will see in the campground where there is a lot less light made by people!

2. Listen to the night sounds. Do you hear animals? The wind in the trees? Try to identify the sounds. Try to remember them so you can see how different the sounds are at the campground.

Backyard Explorer

Before going into the great outdoors to explore, be a nature detective in your own back yard or neighborhood park. Try any of these activities. You might want to break in your new NATURE JOURNAL and describe or sketch what you see. Or be a PHOTOJOURNALIST and start your nature photography collection.

- **Birding.** Look and listen for the birds in your back yard. Using a field guide or on the computer back inside, try to identify what kinds they are.

Psst . . . Kids! Talk to your parents about anything in the night you are afraid of. The night is a very important time for all animals. Night animals (nocturnal) catch food and find companionship in the dark. People and many animals (diurnal) use the night to sleep and recharge for the next day.

Psst . . . Kids! Exercise your new skills as a PHOTOJOURNALIST by taking both close-ups and long shots of plants, critters, and people. Try taking pictures from different angles to see where your shadow is and what the light does to your subject.

- **Bug Hunter.** Look for insects. If you don't see any right away, look underneath stuff. Where else might they be? What kinds did you find?

- **Plant Private Eye.** Look around at the different plants. What are they? Do any serve a specific purpose? What shape are their leaves? Do they have flowers or fruit? What do they feel like? Do they have a smell? Do they attract certain kinds of animals?

- **Animal Detective.** Do you see any animals other than birds or insects? Have any been around? Look for footprints and scat (animal poop). Can you identify what animal they belong to?

Other Pre-Camping Activities!

Try some of these other activities to start learning about camping.

- Go on day hikes.
- Visit a planetarium and learn even more about the night sky!
- Visit a natural history or science museum to learn more about nature.
- Read books about camping, nonfiction or fiction. Some of your favorite characters have had great camping adventures. For

the younger set, you'll find Little Critter, Maisy, Curious George, Fred and Ted (from *Big Dog, Little Dog*), Olivia, Mr. Magee, Amelia Bedelia, and more.

- Find songs online or in songbooks that you can sing around the campfire.
- Find or make up ghost or spooky stories to tell around the campfire, or tell funny or interesting folktales or fairy tales if you don't want it too scary.
- Research famous camping expeditions, and share the stories with your family.

Laugh Time!
Q: How does a bird with a broken wing manage to land safely?
A: With its sparrowchute.

Laugh Time!
Q: What did the big flower say to the small flower?
A: What's up, Bud?

Family Conversation Starters

You'll find questions like these in every chapter. They are here to get everyone in your family reflecting, talking, and listening to one another. Chances are everyone in the family will learn something new about one another and themselves. You'll find a variety of questions, so you can choose ones for kids of any age (2 to 110). Start conversing at home or in the car. Use these conversation starters to suggest other questions. Anyone in the family can make up and ask a conversation starter question!

- What's something you couldn't do when you were younger that you can do now?
- If you were free to do anything you wanted all day, what would you do?
- If you were a season, which season would you be and why?
- What makes you feel loved?
- All of us lose our patience sometimes. Think of a recent time you lost yours. What happened?
- If you were principal of your school, would you change anything? What?
- If you could create a brand-new holiday for the world, what would its traditions be? Describe the what, when, why, and how.

CHAPTER 2
ARRIVAL AT CAMP

You're there! You have pulled into your campsite in the great outdoors, your home away from home for the next few days. This is so exciting! Breathe in that fresh air! It's time to unload the car, set up camp, and explore your new surroundings and all its wonders. Of course the excitement of finally arriving can make unloading the car and setting up feel like just another tedious chore. But with a little imagination and these fun activities, camp prep will set a good tone for the rest of your trip.

> *Climb the mountains and get their good tidings. Nature's peace will flow into you as sunshine flows into trees.*
>
> —John Muir,
> *The Mountains of California*

Psst . . . Kids! You might frown or sneer and say, "What? Unload the car? Set up?" But before you yell "Boring!" we swear that even this process can be fun. If you help out, you can set up your stuff how *you* like it. You'll know where everything is. And you can have a say in where the tent is placed. Being involved will create a sense of togetherness in camp. It feels good when everyone works together. Your parents will appreciate it. (It's always good to get them off to a good start!). At the very least, the setup will go faster with more people chipping in.

Setting Up Camp

Children love to be helpful, well, at least for 5 minutes! Helping to set up is a great way for them to feel some ownership of the experience and more secure in their new surroundings. A few reminders can make it all go better.

Be positive. There are benefits to having a positive attitude about "chores" and adding a bit of fun. Children play. Developmentally, it is how little ones experience and learn about their world. You also are creating lasting impressions. Details fade in memories, but a feeling about an event

Photo by Kevin Meynell

often remains strong throughout the years. Remember acquiring a great gift? Your first car? Our brain creates associations based on experience. You don't want this: *Putting Up Tent = Parents Grumbling and Yelling = Discomfort = Don't Want to Do That Again!*

What is common sense to you may not be common for the kids yet. Speaking of experience, even though we *know* that children have a limited amount of it in five or eight or eleven years compared to an adult, we parents can still forget this fact when we are tired or harried.

Expect mistakes and multiple tries before your helpers actually become helpful. Here is a guide to success (and maintaining family harmony) when a child is helping to set up the tent and campsite, cook and clean, and do anything around camp or is learning a new outdoor activity.

Photo by Leigh Rawdon

Arrival at Camp   23

(Remember, it is a *guide*, perfection not being the goal. We're all human!)

1. Be straightforward and clear with instructions, giving one at a time (especially to young kids).

2. Model or demonstrate the activity, and be patient when they don't understand a "simple" direction (simple for us experienced adults).

3. Allow extra time (patience—deep breath!). Let them repeat a process "unnecessarily" (like lighting a second match for the campfire), and be willing to stop your own task, when needed, to facilitate or watch theirs. (Kids love witnesses!)

4. Let them giggle, fall to the ground, make weird noises, and be frustrated.

5. Authenticate their feelings, and help them move on: "Yeah, that is really frustrating. When you're ready, let's take a deep breath or two together and try again. We can do this, even with frustration."

6. Be flexible, and change the goal if you discover it is too much for your child.

7. Show enthusiasm for the task; model positivity and fun rather than treating it like a chore that has to be completed before fun can begin. The fun has already begun!

8. If setup starts to go long, at least make sure the tent is ready for sleeping and that getting things out for the next meal will be easy. Then go play with the kids!

Laugh Time!
Johnny was hard at work with the broom in his family's tent. His mother came in and said, "That's nice. Are you sweeping out the tent?" "No," Johnny answered. "I'm sweeping out the dirt."

Prepping the Campsite

It's important to have a nice flat, clear area for your tent. Imagine rolling over at night and having a pinecone stick into your back. Ouch! Removing rocks and sticks where the tent is going to go is a necessary part of setup, but that doesn't mean it has to be just another dull chore. Try some of these ideas to make a game out of it:

- **Special sweeper.** Look for a stick or leaves to become your "broom."

- **Collect and sort.** Make a "collection" out of what you clear away, sorting them in piles of like items. It could be all sticks, all rocks, all acorns, or you can sort by size or color or texture.

- **Pictures from debris.** Use debris to make a pattern, picture, statue, or structure on the ground out of the way. You can make it a contest to make the most beautiful "picture," the weirdest structure, or the most creative sculpture. (Everyone gets a prize!)

- **Target practice.** If it's safe to do so, try a little target practice—tossing the rocks and debris to a specific target on the ground away from your tent and people. You can use a stick to mark an X or bull's-eye and try to hit it.

- **Make it a contest.** Who can find and clear the biggest rock or stick, the strangest shaped item, the most colorful? You decide on the categories. The prize could be that everyone else has to follow one command of the winner, such as, "Everyone growl like a bear!"

Tent Setup

Everyone can pitch in when it comes to setting up the tents. Think of it as building your house in the wilderness! Even little hands can help put poles together, put them in the grommets, snap tent poles into place, and (with parental supervision) pound in the stakes. You might want to get a song going while you work, something everybody knows or a repeat-after-me song. (See chapter 8 for some examples.)

> Psst . . . Kids! ALWAYS remove your shoes before going in your tent so you don't track dirt or insects into your "bedroom." This is easy to forget, so make sure you remind your parents as well.

Tent Play

All right! It's time to unzip the door and check out your haven in the great outdoors! These games provide familiarity and positive association for younger campers and test the surface inside to make sure it is flat and clear. They can also keep younger campers busy and safe while parents set up the rest of camp.

- **Wall-to-Wall Roll.** Crawl around the tent in a spiral from the outside in, testing for any rocks or hard spots underneath. If it's all clear, roll yourself from one side of the tent to the other. Roll a ball from one side of the tent to someone sitting on the other side. This tests the plane of the tent (how flat it is on the ground). Report your findings to your parents so you know in which direction to set up sleeping bags. It's no fun to have everyone roll into you at night if you're on the downhill slope!

- **Tent Becomes . . . ?** You are a Native American warrior or princess, a gold prospector in the Wild West, Aladdin, the Lion King, *Frozen*'s Queen Elsa, or a Clash of Clans character. Perhaps you are King of the Campground. In your imaginary role, enter your tent (or cave or castle) to inspect it and do what your character does in your realm. Involve a sibling, friend, or parents or a doll or stuffed animal.

- **Moving Day for the Queen/King.** This is also a great game when moving all your gear inside the tent. You and the other "characters" are preparing the castle for your rule.

Moving In!

Everyone grab your sleeping bags and pillows and set up your "bedroom" in the tent. Younger children might need help setting up their sleeping bags, but they can still find their own places for personal items such as a stuffed animal, doll, book, or headlamp.

If you want to take a more collaborative approach, you can try the assembly-line method. Pretend you are all part of a machine. Move like a robot, and include industrial sound effects as you hand off sleeping bags, pads, and clothes bags to place in the tent.

Exploring the Campsite

You can continue to have your children help you set up camp or send them off to explore on their own. Determine how far your children can go from your campsite to examine their surroundings according to their age, personalities, and your comfort level. They don't have to go far to feel independent. Be clear about the boundaries. Use landmarks. If there are any dangers, like poison oak or mosquitoes, make sure the children are prepared and know how to avoid them, or else simply narrow the initial perimeter for exploration. You can widen it later!

Family Conversation Starters

- What is something you are waiting for, or looking forward to, right now?
- What does it mean to be patient?
- What is your favorite summer food to eat?
- If you had superpowers, what would they be and how would you use them to help people?
- Would you rather go to your school or Hogwarts. Why?
- What's one act of kindness that you have done for someone in the last six months?
- What is one thing you'd like to learn how to do in the next year?
- The poet Maya Angelou once said, "If you don't like something, change it. If you can't change it, change your attitude." What do you think she meant by this? Have you ever had to do this?

CHAPTER 3

POPULAR OUTDOOR ADVENTURES

Welcome to Earth's amusement park! Recreation for the whole family is abundant in our mountains and valleys, our lakes and streams, our beaches and oceans, in and around all campgrounds. There are entire books and collections of books dedicated to each of the recreation activities in this chapter. Those books tell you where to go, what equipment to bring, and how to do each sport or activity. This

Today is your day!
Your mountain is waiting.
So . . . get on your way.
—Dr. Seuss

book will tell you how to make each activity a successful and enjoyable family experience. We want both children and adults to have so much fun that they can't wait for the next camping adventure.

Hiking

These are some tried-and-true tips to making a hiking trip successful when hiking with children.

- **Plan together.** Let kids participate in hike planning.

- **Keep it easy and feature-friendly.** Select a hike that isn't too long or too strenuous. Pick a trail that has some features—a lake, stream, or waterfall,

- **Plan frequent energy/snack stops.** Hiking requires a lot of energy. Energy-sapped kids equal cranky kids. Bring and drink plenty of water.

- **Go your child's pace.** When introducing the activity to younger or new hikers, hike short distances and commit to traveling at a pace comfortable to them.

- **Pick a leader, and then rotate.** Allowing kids to take the lead is empowering and gives you a sense of their pace.

a historical monument, rocks to scramble over, a cave or hollow tree. This will keep kids occupied and give them a goal to reach.

- **Call it an adventure.** For some kids "hiking" is a dirty word implying miles and miles of arduous and pointless walking. Call it an adventure or exploring; emphasize the destination or features along the way.

- **Bring plenty of snacks.** We can't stress this point enough. Bring trail mix, fruit, basically food that gives you energy, packs well, and tastes good. A treat along the trail can take hikers farther. Some parents report that hiking is all about the snacks, even into teen years. If that's what gets them out there, so be it!

Photo by David Rolf

HIKING SONGS

What makes a good hiking song? Anything that keeps a hiker going! This could include everything from classic campfire ditties to pop and rock songs. The best ones have at least one of the following characteristics:

- A cadence good for walking to
- A call-and-response aspect (or louder and softer) or repeat-after-me format
- Room to add your imagination and funny sounds, like "Old MacDonald"
- Humor
- A tune that gets everyone singing together (familiar, catchy, a round, easy to harmonize)

See chapter 8: Songs of the Wild for ideas for hiking-friendly tunes.

- **It's about the journey not the destination.** If your children are more interested in getting down on their hands and knees to explore the undergrowth, then that is the experience for the day. There will always be a next time to cover more ground.

- **Think fun.** Play games, sing songs, look for treasure, and stop to smell the roses or the mountain sage or an ocean breeze.

- **Time is your friend, so plan for lots of it.** Kids are natural explorers and want to pick up and touch everything. This is one of the greatest things about

Photo by Leigh Rawdon

hiking. There's so much of the natural world to discover and examine.

- **Dress for success.** Dress in layers, and wear adequate footwear for the terrain.

- **Prepare for anything.** Along with food and plenty of water, bring sunglasses, hats, sunscreen, a trail guide or map and compass if the trail is new, extra clothing for wet hikers, a headlamp if there's any chance of being back late. Additional kid-friendly supplies include wet wipes or tissues, lip balm, binoculars, magnifying glass, field guides, camera, and safety whistles for each child (and teach them what they are for and when to use them).

- **Practice positive reinforcement.** Tell kids how strong and fast they look. Tell them they remind you of a real explorer!

- **Research.** We're not talking about the trail but your kids. If your child is into a specific video game or TV show, book, toy, or sports team, here's the chance to find out more. What do we adults do on the trail? We chat, and not just about the wildlife along the trail. We talk about our lives. This is an amazing opportunity to engage your child in talking about what they love. You can also use the Family Conversation Starters you'll find in every chapter of this book.

- **Leave no trace.** This is a perfect opportunity to make kids the stewards of our wilderness and public lands. Always bring an extra bag for trash. Pick up anyone else's garbage that you see besides your own!

- **Bring a couple fun extras.** A spray bottle on a hot day is a lot of fun. Bring powdered drink mix to make your water breaks tastier and get them to the next one. Bring M&Ms along with the apples and carrots.

- **Happy kid gear.** Kids love hydration packs. Some like to carry their own stuff in fanny packs or on their belts. If the gear helps, consider it!

- **Keep a sense of wonder.** Try to think like a child on the trail. Look for cool stuff, small stuff, and point it out. Stop to watch a lizard, to smell a tree, to feel a leaf.

- **Be prepared to bail.** You may not make it to your planned destination. If they've had enough, it's okay to turn around and head back.

How to Poop in the Woods

You're on the trail, and nature calls. It's part of the adventure! Potty talk is okay here. Once the kids get the hang of it, they might even enjoy this element of being in the great outdoors and look for a rock with a view. But when they are getting used to it or still squeamish about it, you can make the experience a good one for them.

Give it a creative name. This takes embarrassment and tension out of the

experience. "I have to use the facili-trees." Or you can have different code names for #1 and #2. The family can decide on them. Phrases could be something like: "I have to go chase a squirrel" or "I have to go chase a cougar."

Go with your child to find a spot. If it is dark, do not go too far from camp, and always take a flashlight with you. (General advice is to find a place *at least* 100 feet from camp and the trail and 200 feet from water sources.)

Find a sturdy object if possible, like a secure rock. This allows your child to use it for support. Or if they are really little, you can hold their hands while they squat. Encourage them or assist them in digging a hole and covering it afterwards. (The hole, by the way, should be no more than 6 inches deep. Bacteria that break down this waste don't live deeper than that.)

To TP or not TP. The most environmentally friendly method is to use leaves and sticks rather than toilet paper for wiping. If using TP, most naturalists recommend carrying the used paper out with you, preferably double-bagged. (Make the TP caddy, described on page 13.) You decide what works for your family.

Make it easy for your children to wash or sanitize their hands.

Night Hiking

You'll experience an entirely different landscape on a night hike. You don't need to go far. If you have young hikers, a half mile or even a few hundred yards in the dark can feel far. Choose a well-trodden path, a familiar trail, or even campground road so you feel confident and sure-footed. It's a good idea to start during dusk when you still have some light; that way part of the experience is to watch the change in light, to take in crepuscular (twilight) sounds as well as nocturnal ones, and to see the stars appear in the sky. It also helps your eyes adjust to the dark. Bring water, a snack, and a flashlight for all. If possible, make the end of your journey a place away from light noise where you can really take in the night sky. On the way back, make sure all hikers have a flashlight or can see where they are walking. Stop now and then and turn off your lights.

Geocaching

Geocaching (JEE-oh-kash-ing) is a great way to turn a hike into a modern-day treasure hunt. You simply download a geocaching app onto your smartphone or use a handheld Global Positioning System (GPS) unit. You can start with the free Geocaching Intro App. Get ready to find hidden objects by means of GPS coordinates! There are millions of geocaches around the world. Inside each cache you will find at least a logbook to sign. Larger caches also contain various inexpensive trinkets for trade. It is a good idea to pack a few "treasures" of your own to replace the ones you take from larger caches. You'll find caches along hiking trails and near campgrounds, but you can continue the adventure at home, geocaching in your own neighborhood.

What to bring. Bring a pen and basic hiking supplies (snacks, water, etc.). It is a good idea to bring along a compass, map, and extra batteries in case your GPS device fails. Many geocaches are off the beaten track so that people won't take them by mistake. Wear long pants and close-toed shoes, and be prepared for some minor bushwhacking. If you have a camera, add to the fun by photographing your geocachers and upload the picture on the app or geocaching.com.

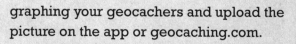

- Pick a time of day for your walk when birds are most plentiful. Early morning and late afternoon are especially good times.

- Keep quiet while you walk. Move slowly, and try to blend in with your surroundings. Try sitting in one place for a while.

Laugh Time!
Q: How do you catch a unique bird?
A: Unique up on it.

- Look up into trees. Look in shrubs. Listen. If there is a body of water nearby, walk there. You will likely see other kinds of birds there.

Once you get the hang of it, you can even create your own geocache for others to find.

Birding

Birding is a favorite hobby of millions of people all over the world. You can start out as a birder with nothing but an observant eye. To really get the most out of birding, though, get a pair of binoculars and a bird field guide for your area. You can even familiarize yourself with birdcalls. Time to identify some cool feathered friends with your family!

- Some of the best birding is in open-water wetlands, where you can see water birds easily and note their field marks and behaviors.

- Bring along snacks and sunscreen.

- Really young birders can enjoy using a pair of empty toilet paper rolls for pretend binoculars.

- If you have a field guide, get it out and try to identify the species you are spotting. If you don't, make the activity meaningful by discussing with your family the song, behavior, appearance, and location of the birds you see.

- Celebrate every observation and discovery. It doesn't matter how many

birds you see. Sometimes watching one bird for a long time yields the greatest rewards.

- In your NATURE JOURNAL, describe your bird and birding experience. You might write about where and when you spotted the bird, what it was doing, and its color, size, and features. Try sketching it. Back in the campground you'll have more time to look up the birds you saw in a field guide. Be a PHOTOJOURNALIST and take pictures of the birds and their habitats. You can paste the pictures into your journal at home.

Bicycling

If you're going for a family bike ride, many of the same tips for hiking apply to this activity:

- Bring plenty of snacks and water, clothes for unexpected weather.

- Choose your destination ahead of time and be aware of the mileage and terrain, making sure it is achievable for everyone in your family to ride.

- Take breaks, and enjoy the journey.

oiled, and make sure their bikes are ready to go. The kids will feel more ownership of the experience, and the trip won't be delayed by unexpected bike maintenance. Make sure everyone has a helmet and doesn't wear loose pants or a skirt that could get caught in the chain.

Sit down as a family before the ride and discuss ground rules. Parents, make it clear if you don't want anyone riding more than a few hundred

Here are a few more things that can go a long way to making your ride smooth and magical.

Try to prepare the bicycles the day before the ride or earlier in the day. Under supervision, parents can make it a family project for the kids to check the air in their tires, make sure their chains are

yards away from the rest of the family or if it's important to keep a slow pace to accommodate a young child or older family member. Discussing these expectations ahead of time can eliminate stress, tantrums, and general annoyance on the ride.

Swimming

Swimming is often the first thing we think of when we imagine an outdoor family vacation. Take all safety precautions as suggested by the Red Cross or Kids Health Organization (easily found online), and then use these tips for added success.

Reapply sunscreen often. Consider bringing goggles for the kids. Goggles allow kids to see and explore underwater better, and many provide UV protection as well. Because swimmers are in water, it is easy to forget to *drink* water. Make sure everyone takes hydrating and reenergizing breaks.

If the water is really cold, don't force kids to swim. They may be happier wading or exploring on the shore or making sand castles. Set up a "drying or warming station" on sand or a big slab of stone, surfaces that absorbs the sun's heat. If it's a hot day, find a shady spot for breaks. And always be ready for a change in the weather by keeping clothes dry and having layers.

It's awesome if one of the features of your campground or hike is a swimming hole, lake, or stream. Inspect the shore and depth so you know how to guide your family for safety. Beware of river currents, and research any ocean beaches before swimming in the tides.

Photos by David Rolf

Wading in a Rocky Shore. If you know the shore will be rocky, outfit your kids in aqua socks or water shoes. If you don't have such gear, model rock stepping and guide your kids. That way, you can test for sharp rocks and help kids be more sure-footed and learn how to watch their step, good lifelong skills. It could be frustrating at first for any tenderfoot, so be supportive and patient. Don't let kids swim in weeds and grass, where a leg or arm could get tangled.

Water Critters. When swimming in a natural body of water, you are likely to encounter critters that live there, especially bugs. Try to acquaint your kids with the animals, especially if they are shaky about sharing the water. Kids can have a ball getting their toes nibbled by minnows once they know they have nothing to fear.

If you have a bucket or container or even a plastic baggie, you might be able to safely catch a water bug to examine and then let go. It's a wonderful opportunity to teach kids to be respectful of a habitat and the creatures that live there. Be content to look at any fragile water habitats, such as ponds and marshes, rather than enter them.

Make Your Own Floatie. Didn't bring an inflatable raft or inner tube? Never fear! You can use your sleeping pad. Works great! But only use it when you have enough sunshine and time to dry it before bedtime. And since sleeping pads are a lot more expensive than a pool toy, keep them away from rocks and rougher play. If you're out boating and stop for a swim, the

Photos by David Rolf

Boating

There are so many wonderful family experiences to be had on the water. Whether you venture out in a canoe or a speedboat or try a paddleboard, here are some tips for a fun excursion in a watercraft. As always, bring lots of food and water. If you're going to be out for a long time, consider bringing cards or music. Applying sunscreen or wearing a hat is important, and make sure kids are adequately dressed for all conditions (heat, rain, cold) and also for the water before leaving the dock. This may include waterproof articles and always means nonskid deck shoes. A good, well-fitting life vest is worth the price.

kids may enjoy bobbing around in their life vests.

Give each family member an onboard task or job. Family boating responsibilities can range from going over a pre-departure checklist to serving as a lookout and can instill children with confidence and make them very present in the moment. It's a wonderful opportunity to work together as a team. Teach kids (or learn all together) about boat terminology and safety.

Have a destination or goal activity. It could be to find the best skiing spot or fishing spot on the lake, to find a rock for sunbathing and picnicking or jumping in the lake, or to find a beach for building sand castles.

For very young sailors, think about the length of time on the water and the weather conditions. If renting a party boat, get one with a canopy to provide some shade. A fishing boat with a small kiddy cabin will provide a place your little one can take a nap and get out of the sun. If you're a long time out in a canoe, kayak, or raft, take more breaks on shore.

If rafting, make sure you have an experienced guide for any rapids rated above Class II. Set expectations, explain instructions and emergency procedures clearly before setting off, and choose a river that's appropriate to the age of the children and not too scary. You want them to feel confident about the next time.

Have fun on the water!

Beachcombing

Seashells have been collected for thousands of years. Many cultures have used various types of shells as decorations, jewelry, and money and even ground them up to be used in medicines. Some beaches also have sea glass—what started as broken bottles but was shaped smooth and pretty by the sea. Enjoy an afternoon of beachcombing with the family.

Research ahead of time to make sure you can take things from the beach. In a state or national park or a preserve,

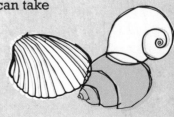

lots of shells or if it will take searching to find some beauties. When hunting for shells, ensure that the original inhabitant of the shell is not still inside. Shells are often found in the shallow waters near the beach and along the beach where the tide has forced the shells onto the shore.

Come equipped for sun, sand, and water. Besides your water and food, bring a bucket or bag for each beachcomber. Consider bringing a guidebook to look up what kind of animal left each shell.

Saving Your Shells. You'll need to clean and preserve the shell to remove its sea smell and to ensure it lasts a long time. First remove any loose debris or sand with a cotton cloth. Next soak the shell in a solution of half bleach and half water until the outer covering (periostracum) can be brushed off. Use a toothbrush and a toothpick to clean out any cracks, bumps, or whorls. If desired, file any sharp or jagged edges with an emery board. Shine up your shell with a bit of baby oil and a cotton cloth.

Using Your Shells. Put small shells in the bottom of a clear flower vase before

everything must stay where it is. Less-populated beaches often offer more shells. Shells don't necessarily have to come from saltwater beaches. Mussels that produce tiny shells inhabit many freshwater lakes. Find out what to expect, if there will be

adding flowers to give the room a beach feel. Use larger shells as decorative accents on bookshelves or windowsills. Drill holes in smaller shells to make mobiles or necklaces.

Fishing

Fishing with the family can be a lot of fun, but it can take a lot of patience on the part of parents, especially with young and brand-new anglers. Being patient is the number-one rule for making fishing a successful experience.

Don't expect to do much fishing yourself. Take enjoyment in helping your children, rigging lines, and being in a beautiful place with your family. You will likely need more patience than you can imagine. Lost lures, knots, dropped worms. It all happens. The key is to positively reinforce your children's attempt to learn to fish and shake off the minor setbacks. If they sense any frustration on your part, they're likely to emulate it. Stay positive and encouraging.

Time and Location. Find a place to fish where snags are less likely. New casters can easily tangle and snag lines. They generally have a hard time leaving the pole alone for long, wanting to frequently reel it in to check the bait and cast again. It's a new and exciting experience.

Photo by David Rolf

Encourage and model good fishing habits and techniques, but let them keep casting too. For younger anglers, consider taking off the hook for a while so they can cast over and over without snagging. If you catch a fish on your rig, bring them over to help reel it in so they will be part of the catch. Bring plenty of extra rigging and good tools to help you rig up new lines quickly. **And bring a sense of humor!** If you have several young anglers on the shore, it can be a lot of work for you but pretty exciting for the kids.

Photo by David Rolf

should any tangles occur. You want a push-button model for beginners.

Supplies to Bring. Make sure to bring water, plenty of snacks, a book or cards, the child's NATURE JOURNAL and this book to keep them occupied! Have them dress in layers and wear a hat. Bring bug repel- lent and sunscreen. If you are shore casting, consider bringing folding camp chairs or cushions

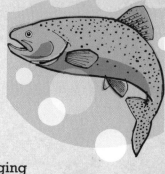

For optimum enjoyment, it is best to go when there is little wind and it's not too cold so that it's more comfortable. It's also when you are most likely to catch a fish! It is more exciting to fish during early morning and late afternoon because you are more likely to see fish jump out of the water to get bugs and make ripples on the water.

Equipment. Children of all ages do best with a spinning rod. The closed-face reels are easy to use—and easy to fix

Laugh Time!
Q: What do you call a fish without any eyes?
A: Fsh.

Photo by David Rolf

to sit on. On a boat or near deep water, always have life jackets for your little ones.

Safety First. Before fishing, make sure the kids know this golden fishing rule: Watch where the hook is at all times. If your children are walking with a fishing pole from your campsite or your car to the water, take off the rigging or make sure the hook is securely fastened.

Not Just Fishing. If your children are suddenly happier playing with rocks than fishing for a while,

Photo by David Rolf

let them play or move to a new fishing spot. Plan time to hunt for frogs, tadpoles, worms, or snails. Expect that they'll want to get their feet (and possibly everything else) wet.

Practice. If possible, have your kids practice casting on a clear area of grass or dirt without a hook before going fishing. Once on the water, they may be too excited to pay attention to a fishing lesson.

Release or Keep. Kids usually want to keep anything they catch. If you are releasing the fish, establish this ahead of time, explaining that it gives the fish a chance to grow, reproduce, and perhaps return when it is bigger. Or explain that if you don't plan on eating it, it's best to let it go. If the fish is large enough and you are willing to clean and cook it, this is a good lesson about the realities of where our food comes from. **If they don't catch a fish,** explain that catching a fish isn't the only goal of this outing. It may not even happen. Set expectations early and straightforwardly.

Guided Adventures

Beyond what you read about here, there are some pretty exciting outdoor adventures to be had that require a guide with a high level of expertise. If your family is up for it, consider an organized tour of rock climbing, spelunking, or whitewater rafting. If booking one of these adventures, make sure it is appropriate for the ages of your kids and that everyone in the family wants to do it. If they are still too young, wait a few years. It's something to look forward to.

Family Conversation Starters

- If you could have any adventure, what would it be and where would you go?
- If you were an explorer, would you prefer to explore on land, in water, or in the sky? Why?
- If you woke up tomorrow and could do one thing that you can't do right now, what would it be?
- How do you feel about bugs?
- What do you do when you are afraid?
- What would you do if you made the rules at home?
- If you could live during another time in history, when would that be? Why?

CHAPTER 4

EXPLORING NATURE

To be a nature explorer, your first and primary tool is curiosity. Start with that, and the rest will come naturally. All the activities in this section involve exploring your surroundings in fascinating, focused, and fun ways using your senses. Each is enhanced by two other important elements to becoming an explorer or scientist: information and imagination.

Explorers make discoveries, and there's no more exciting and memorable way of learning than through discovery. Sharing this with the people you love can

There is a way that nature speaks, that land speaks. Most of the time we are simply not patient enough, quiet enough to pay attention to the story.

—Linda Hogan, Native American poet

Photo by Kevin Meynell

make it even better! Go out and discover and share the world of nature, your world!

Exploring with Your Senses

These activities use the different senses to experience nature in deeper, more meaningful ways. All can be adjusted for ages 2 to 102.

I Heard That!

Do you hear what I hear? Listen carefully!

Stand quietly in the middle of the campsite and listen to the sounds around you. Now close your eyes. What do you hear? Can you identify any animals? Do you hear sounds made by people? The wind? Are there patterns to the sounds? Try this on the trail. Try this in the forest, in a clearing, and near water.

- **NATURE JOURNAL.** Note the time, and write down everything you hear in your Nature Journal. Can you imagine these sounds in a song or the soundtrack for a story? Write a story about one or several of the sounds. Try listening later from the same place. What has changed?
- **Turn it into a game.** Listen with another camper. Set an amount of time, like 2 minutes, and compare what you heard.

- **Listen like a deer.** Try cupping your hands around your ears forward and backward. Then one each. Deer have far better hearing than we do; they also have complex muscles that enable their ears to revolve like radar without any movement of the head. This allows deer to place the direction and distance of sounds with pinpoint accuracy.

- **PHOTOJOURNALIST.** Take a short video, panning your surroundings to capture the sounds. Once back home, you can watch your video to remember those sounds.

Listening for Echoes

Hello! Hello. Echo! Echo. Echoes are fascinating and fun to test. Try to find places that echo.

Understanding sound will help you find echoes. Sound is actually little moving vibrations or waves sent through the air that translate into noises when our ears pick them up. An echo is what happens when these vibrations bounce off a surface as they travel and play back again a second time (or even a third, fourth, or more times!). That's why an echo is more likely to happen when the sound has a lot of surfaces to bounce off.

Where do you find echoes in nature? Look for vertical rock faces over open spaces. Caves, canyons, and rocky ravines may have an echo. You might be able to find a place where you can hear multiple echoes. Back at home after camping, you might find echoes by calling into the bottom of a well, by a building, or toward the walls of an enclosed or empty room.

When you get to a place that you think might have an echo, try calling

out. Move your position to see if you can create multiple echoes or change the time delay of the echo. Try speaking and singing. Record the sound of the echo on a smartphone or describe it in your NATURE JOURNAL or be a PHOTOJOURNALIST and take a

picture of the place where you stood to get the echoes. Can you figure out from where the sound waves are reflecting? How long is the time delay of the echo? Was-was making-making an-an echo-echo fun-fun?

Bats and Echoes. Bats rely heavily on echoes. They rarely run into anything and find insects to eat using echolocation [eh-koh-lo-KAY-shun]. They send out sound waves through their mouth or nose. When the sound hits an object, an echo comes back. A bat can identify an object by the sound of the echo and can even tell the size, shape, and texture of the object, even a tiny insect, from its echo. Most bats use echolocation to navigate in the dark and find food.

Touching the Earth

Can't touch this . . . actually you can! Feel all the textures of nature.

Gently explore your surroundings by touch, feeling the texture of a tree or leaf, the temperature of the earth, the delicateness of a flower petal, the wetness of dew on the grass, the hard shell of a beetle.

Note the time, and write down everything you touch in your NATURE JOURNAL. You might try drawing the items you touch, describing them, or taking pictures of them. Is there something else that feels similar? Try touching the same things later. What has changed? If you feel like it, write a story about one or several of the things you feel.

PHOTOJOURNALIST. Try to capture the texture of the object in a photo by playing with the light, taking a close-up,

or setting it in contrast against some other object or on your hand.

Warning: Make sure to identify and avoid touching any poison oak or ivy or insects or critters that might cause harm. Supervise small children carefully.

Meteorologist

Very rarely are we aware of the air around us. Feel the air around you. Does it feel moist? (That's humidity.) Dry? Warm? Cold? Is it constantly changing as the sun comes and goes? What do you think the temperature might be? Take a guess. Look up at the sky. If there are clouds, are they moving and how fast? Make a prediction for the night's temperature and tomorrow's weather.

The Smells of Nature

Stop and smell the flowers . . . no, really, stop and smell the flowers, the trees, the plants, the soil, the creek, even stones in the sun.

There are so many amazing smells in nature. Pleasant and stinky smells too! There is much to explore when you use your nose. Have you ever stopped to smell the bark of a pine tree? Some Nature Explorers say it smells like vanilla or maple, or butterscotch, or even cocoa. Locate sap on a tree. Why do you think it smells that way? Smelling plants, you are likely to find natural herbs like sage. Does having a smell help a plant to survive? Invite family members to smell what you've found and find some smells of their own to share.

NATURE JOURNAL: Write down the object, a physical description, and its smell. Besides adjectives like *sweet, savory, citrusy, pungent, mild,* and *earthy,* a great way to describe smells is by using **similes** (SIM-uh-lees), comparing something unfamiliar with something more familiar using the words *like* or *as.* **Examples:** It smells like Christmas morning. It smells like the lawn freshly mowed.

PHOTOJOURNALIST: Okay, you can't capture smells with a camera, but you can still take pictures of things with really good, really bad, or otherwise really memorable smells. Back at home, you can label them as such or print them out and paste them in your Nature Journal.

The Sights of Nature

Use keen observation to see all the nature around you.

Sit or stand in one place and look around. What do you see? Is there any movement? Is there light and dark? Are there a variety of colors, shapes, and sizes of objects around you? Notice anything you didn't see before? Write what you see in your NATURE JOURNAL. Be a PHOTOJOURNALIST with some of your favorite sights, both close up and far away.

The Colors of Nature

Challenge yourself and others to find every color of the rainbow around you while you hike. That could include a rainbow! Make it a Scavenger Hunt game (see page 110). Take notes in your NATURE JOURNAL.

Family Conversation Starters

- Who is your best friend? Why?
- What is one way that you take care of yourself?
- Do you know the story about how your parents met?
- What would motivate you to try new foods or activities?
- What do you think the future will be like?
- What is your favorite kind of weather?
- Have you ever participated in a tradition from a culture other than your own? What was it? How did you like it?
- If you had the chance to leave Earth, would you? What are some things you'd miss the most?
- Albert Einstein said, "Look! Look! Look deep into nature and you will understand everything." What do you think he meant?
- Black Elk, a Sioux medicine and holy man, said, "One should pay attention to even the smallest crawling creature for these too may have a valuable lesson to teach us." What can they teach us?

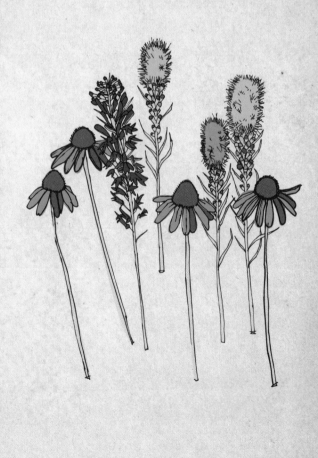

The Patterns of Nature

Art often imitates nature, and it is said that imitation is the highest form of flattery! This includes patterns. In nature you can find interesting patterns everywhere: the rings on the end of a fallen log, the cluster of leaves on a bush, the ripples of wind on water. Look for patterns around you. Write about them, sketch them in your NATURE JOURNAL or try to capture them with a close-up as a PHOTOJOURNALIST. Challenge other campers to find patterns of their own.

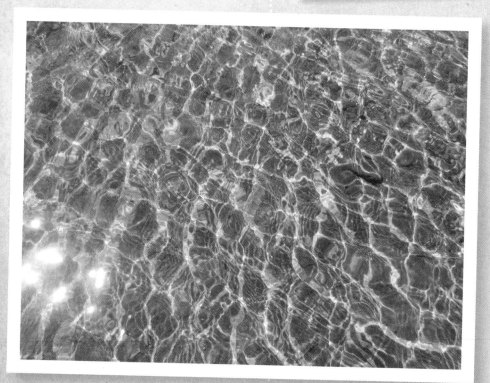

The Shapes of Nature

Nature presents us with many shapes! Why are leaves and trees and flowers shaped the way they are? Some scientists study the shape of nature to better understand our world. They use mathematics. Artists study the shape of nature for its beauty. What shapes do you see? Are any unusual or unique? How close to a triangle or square or circle are some of the shapes? Can you draw them in your NATURE JOURNAL? Or capture them as a PHOTOJOURNALIST?

Did You Know?

The Shakedown on Shapes in Nature

When scientists look at the shapes of nature, they use mostly two types of mathematics. They look at shapes in terms of geometry (jee-OM-i-tree), the study and measurements of points, lines, shapes, and space (length, area, and volume). Geometry is one of the oldest studies of mathematics. One theory used to describe nature is fractal geometry. A fractal is a never-ending pattern. A mountain or a tree could be considered a fractal. (Check out fractals online at home; they can be very beautiful!)

Scientists also use topology (tuh-POL-uh-jee), a type of geometry that looks at spaces and shapes. In topology, you can look at any kind of shape with a space and manipulate the shape any way you wish, but as long as the space remains unchanged, it remains the same mathematically. So, if you take a string in the shape of a circle and pull it out at four points, you get a rectangle or square, but the space inside is the same. For another example, imagine a doughnut made of clay. It has a hole, which is unchangeable, but you can shift and smooth the clay into the shape of a coffee mug. The doughnut hole becomes the coffee cup handle, and the number of holes and its size is preserved. The doughnut and the coffee mug have the same topology. Math can be weird and fun! Using these principles, scientists look for answers to questions like "How did this leaf get this shape?" And even "What is the shape of the universe?" Whoa!

15 Minutes of Sitting Still

You may ask. "Seriously?! Sitting still for 15 minutes is fun?" The answer is that this activity is simple and can be extraordinary.

Find a beautiful place in nature—a rock or a soft patch of ground in a meadow or forest to sit on. Sit down. Set a timer for 15 minutes, or ask someone to keep track of time for you. Others can be sitting still nearby or, if you feel safe, out of sight but close by so they can come get you in 15 minutes. Stay in one place, and see what you see! You may start to squirm. You may feel the first pangs of boredom or other emotions. Ride it out and look around you. The moment is yours. Write about the experience afterward (not during) in your NATURE JOURNAL.

Tip to parents: Make sure kids are old enough, make sure the spot they choose is safe, and be sure to fetch them in 15 minutes, not more, so they don't have to think about time and know they can rely on you.

Exploring with Imagination

These activities help you to see nature in a whole new light. It's no wonder that inventors and artists throughout the ages have been inspired by our natural world.

Letter Search

If you look carefully, you can find the entire alphabet in nature! It's true! Perhaps some branches will crisscross to form a capital *A*. A chipped rock might look like a *B*. See if you can find every letter of the alphabet in the world around you. As a PHOTOJOURNALIST, take close-ups that clearly show the letter.

When you get home, you can print out and combine your pictures to spell names and words!

Imagination Observation

Did you ever notice how a branch can sometimes look like the body of a person? Or a stump can resemble an animal? Or a knot or burl in a tree can look like the face of a gnome? Or a clump of moss can look like a bed for a fairy or a tired mouse? Are the trees doing a dance when the wind moves them?

Look around at your surroundings. Can you see shapes, shadows, or even movements that remind you of other things? Share these with a fellow camper, challenge them to see what you see and find some imaginative shapes of their own. As a PHOTOJOURNALIST, see if you can get just the right angle and frame the picture to capture the scene. Consider writing down what you see in your NATURE JOURNAL and let your observations inspire stories, drawings, or questions.

Cloud Dreaming

Are there clouds in the sky today? Try **Imagination Observation** with the clouds. Find a nice place to lie down and look up at the sky. (Remember to never look directly into the sun!)

Look at the clouds. Do their shapes resemble animals or objects to you? You might see a train or a bunny, an exploding volcano, a lion roaring, a fish swimming. You never know! This is a great one for the entire family while taking a break on a day hike. Besides being imaginative, it's quite relaxing. Sometimes what you see can be pretty funny! This is another opportunity to use your NATURE JOURNAL or be a PHOTOJOURNALIST. In your journal, use similes to describe the clouds or let them inspire a story. Try to capture those clouds and their shapes in a picture.

Boldly Amazing Boulder Stories

You can figure out the history of large rocks by their location and situation!

How did boulders get to where they are? Look at larger rocks and try to figure out their stories. To move a giant boulder takes a lot of energy, a lot more than to move a tiny sand particle. Which is more likely to move a giant boulder: a trickling stream or a raging river? If you see a massive boulder in the middle of a dry creekbed, you know that there had to be a whole lot of water rushing through it at one point. Where did gravity play a role in placing a

boulder? What else can move boulders? Ancient ice flows (moving glaciers) once moved a lot of debris. Are the rocks volcanic? Perhaps they landed there, spewed by a once-active volcano. This activity can be fascinating and full of discovery.

When you're not sure of the answer, you can make up a story too! Consider writing down your observations in your NATURE JOURNAL. Be a PHOTOJOURNALIST and capture the boulder in pictures.

Scene for a Story

While exploring, look for an intriguing setting. In books and plays a "setting" is a place, a time, and the conditions when some action takes place. In nature there are

many wonderful settings where a story can take place—deep in a forest, high on a plateau before a beautiful view, in a sun-drenched meadow. Identify such places and what scene or story you can imagine taking place there. Capture it as a PHOTOJOURNALIST or in your NATURE JOURNAL.

Exploring by Searching

Now you're off to discover new and interesting parts of nature. Like a detective, you will discover clues and patterns and start to identify the natural truth. You will notice things you normally might not notice. Get out your magnifying glass, Sherlock!

Rock Hunting

Turn your hike into a rock hunt. Become a rock and mineral hound, and start collecting!

Supplies: Rocks, a container for displaying your rocks, a rock and mineral guidebook (optional)

No two rock collections are alike, because no two rocks are alike. They are unique, just like people. To start, just look for rocks you think are cool. Look for rocks of different colors, textures, and consistencies. Organize them

by these categories and examine them. As you learn more about rocks and minerals, you might want to concentrate on finding certain types and purchasing rock and mineral guidebooks.

Identifying the rock type:

There are three categories of rocks: sedimentary, metamorphic, and igneous. Which type is your rock?

- **Sedimentary** rocks are created through thousands or even millions of years of pressure. Bits of rocks, minerals, dirt, seashells, bones, and other debris are pressed together. So sedimentary rocks often look like they have layers. Those more recently formed can be broken apart with your hands or by hitting them with another rock or hammer. Examples are sandstone, shale, conglomerate, limestone, and coal.

- **Metamorphic** rocks are created by pressure and heat, often from Earth's magma, so they are more permanently fused. (From Greek, *meta* means "change," and *morph* means "form.") Forces and time have brought these rocks to the surface. Examples are slate, schist, gneiss, and marble.

- **Igneous** rocks formed out of the cooling of molten rock material, magma beneath the Earth and lava on the surface. Examples that formed below the Earth's surface are diorite, gabbro, and granite. Examples that formed above the Earth's surface are basalt, obsidian, and pumice.

Laugh Time!
Dr. Watson: Holmes, what kind of rock is this?
Sherlock Holmes: Why that's sedimentary, my dear Watson.

Describing Your Rocks!

Number or label each rock, and in your NATURE JOURNAL write down the number and add a description. Scientists often call this cataloging. Where did you find the rock? At what time and on what date? Next, record the five properties visible in each rock:

1. **Color.** Is it red, orange-red, blue-green, gray?

2. **Texture.** How does the rock feel to the touch?

3. **Luster.** How shiny is it?

   You can use this chart to help you describe the rock's luster:

   - *Dull* — a nonreflective surface
   - *Earthy* — the look of dirt or dried mud
   - *Fibrous* — the look of fibers
   - *Greasy* — the look of grease
   - *Metallic* — the look of metals
   - *Silky* — the look of silk, similar to fibrous but more compact
   - *Vitreous* — the look of glass
   - *Waxy* — the look of wax

4. **Shape.** Is it square, round, or rectangular?

5. **Pattern.** Does it have a pattern? Is it striped? Speckled?

   If you do this, you are officially an amateur rock hound!

How to collect and display your rocks:

Organization is key when starting any collection. Serious rock and mineral hounds use special boxes and labels. While camping, consider repurposing used food packages or containers from your camping kitchen to collect and display your rocks and minerals: an egg carton or a cut-open cereal or cracker box. You can create nests for each rock out of paper towels or toilet paper.

Photo by Kevin Meynell

Variation

For very young children, keep it simple. Collect a bunch of rocks and, in a clear space on the table or ground, sort them by size. Then sort them by color. Then sort them by shape. Ask your kids if they can think of other ways to sort them?

Seed Explorer

Plants are truly amazing in a lot of ways. One of the most amazing ways is how they deposit or disperse their seeds. Within every seed lives a tiny plant, an embryo that stays dormant until it is in the right conditions to grow. There are so many unique designs of seeds that allow them to travel near or far to find those right conditions and survive. See if you can discover different kinds of seeds and how different plants deposit or disperse their seeds. Design your own seed! (See the activity Plant a Seed, page 101.)

Supplies:

- Ziplock bag or container with lid
- Old, large socks
- Plate
- Glue, tape, markers (optional)
- Books or plant field guides about seeds and plants (optional)
- Cup (optional)

Go on a seed walk. Get something to collect seeds in, preferably something that closes so that seeds don't fall out. There are two ways to take a seed walk; try both. First, walk around looking for and collecting as many different seeds as you can. You only need a few of each type. Second, find a meadow or field. Put large socks on over your shoes and walk around a meadow. Take off any seeds stuck to your socks, and put them in your container.

Did You Know?

The Scoop on Seeds

The biggest seed in the world is the coco de mer (*Lodoicea maldivica*), also known as the double coconut or love nut. It grows only in the Seychelles, a group of islands in the Indian Ocean. It weighs up to 38 pounds and is the shape of a human bottom!

The smallest seeds in the world are those of epiphytic orchids (family Orchidaceae) in the tropical rain forest. Some seeds are only 1/300th of an inch and weigh only 1/35,000,000th of an ounce. They are too small to be seen by the naked eye.

The record for the oldest seed ever grown is a 2,000-year-old date palm recovered near the Dead Sea, bordering Jordan and Israel. When botanists (plant scientists) germinated them, one of the seeds grew.

Three seeds feed most of the world: rice, wheat, and maize (corn).

Seeds that can fly, like those of the sycamore tree and dandelion, may have given people the idea for helicopters and parachutes. The idea for Velcro came from a burdock seed. Swiss engineer Georges de Mestral returned with his dog from a hunting trip in the Swiss Alps and saw that his pant legs and his dog's hair were covered in burrs from the burdock plant. As an engineer, he naturally began to wonder how exactly the seeds stuck so effectively to his pants and his dog. He examined the burrs under a microscope and discovered that they had very tiny hooks, which allowed the seeds to catch onto fabrics, which have tiny loops. The word *Velcro* is a portmanteau of the two French words *velours* ("velvet") and *crochet* ("hook").

Sort your seeds. Dump your collection onto a plate or tray. Sort the seeds based on color, shape, size, and other differences.

Discover how each seed moves. Once the seeds are sorted, try to figure out how each seed moves in order to be planted. Go through each different type of seed and conduct experiments. **Examples:** If you blow on it, does it fly through the air? If you put it in a cup of water, does it float? For how long? Did this one stick to your socks or to your clothes? What would happen if an animal walked through that field and then traveled over the next hill?

Create Your Collection

Glue or tape an example of each seed in your NATURE JOURNAL or onto a sheet of paper. Label each seed with:

- The name or type of plant. If you don't know its name, include a brief description as well as where you found it (forest, meadow, shade, light, on hill, etc.).

- How it is dispersed and how you know this.
- Any other thoughts or questions you have about the seed.
- Sketch the plant or seed and/or leave room to paste in a photo of the plant.

Share your discoveries with the family PHOTOJOURNALIST. Take pictures of the different plants and seeds. Make a video demonstrating their seed dispersal systems.

Bug Hunter

It's time to look at insects, those amazing creatures that make up the majority population on our planet! If you've got a commercial bug cage with you, great! If not, make your own.

Supplies:

- A made or bought bug house
- A cup or stiff paper (paper plate) for collecting
- Tweezers and a magnifying glass (optional)

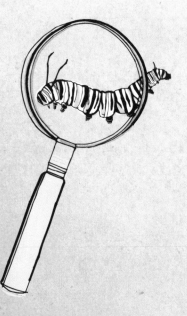

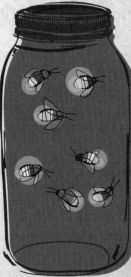

Q: What is on the ground and also a hundred feet in the air?
A: A centipede on its back!

Laugh Time!

1. **Finding Bugs.** Where can you find bugs? Try in decomposing wood, under rocks, or around flowers. Where else can you look? Unless you or your parents have some bug know-how, stay away from bees, wasps, and spiders.

2. **Capturing Bugs.** Place one cup in front of the insect. Use the other cup or cardboard to gently slide or push the insect into the first cup. It is okay if you also scoop up dirt or wood particles. This material is either food or shelter to the insects. Be patient so you don't injure the bug.

3. **Bug House.** Cover a bowl or cup with plastic wrap secured with a rubber band, twine, or tape. Poke holes in the top for air. Make sure to put wood-land debris that you find near the bug into the house. (You can use repur-posed packages for a house too and a splatter screen for a roof.)

Bug versus Insect

Is this question bugging you: What is the difference between a bug and an insect, or do the two words mean the same?

We tend to use the word "bug" loosely for any very small creature with legs. However, a true bug is one type of insect. True bugs, such as beetles, usually have tough forewings and lack teeth. True bugs have a stylet (a mouth shaped like a straw) that they use to suck juices from plants. Insects, like bees and mosquitoes, have three-part bodies, usually two pairs of wings, and three pairs of legs. Arthropods (spiders, ticks, centipedes, and the like) are in a separate category from bugs and insects.

But you can still call them all bugs! It has become a common term for all these little critters.

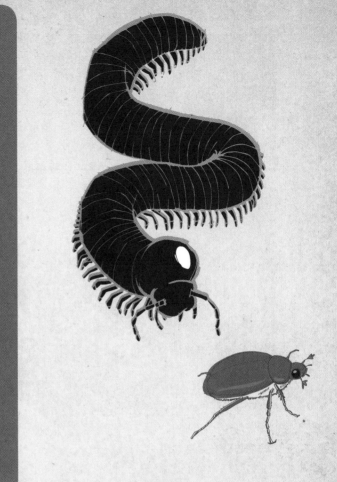

4. **Observation.** Now it's time to check out your bug's behavior and characteristics. Note them in your NATURE JOURNAL. You might want to draw the bug. For some fun, write what the insect would say if it could talk. If it could dance, what kind of dance would it do? Be a PHOTOJOURNALIST (or in this case a shutterbug!) and capture that insect in pictures or video.

> Psst...Kids! Never bring your bug house into the tent. That's a place for campers only!

5. **Releasing the Bug.** Try not to harm the insect. After a short stay in the bug house, release it gently back to its home by pouring it out of the cup back where you found it. You can scoot it out slowly with a leaf or stick if need be.

Animal Detective

Who else lives in your part of the woods? If you can't see those elusive mammals or reptiles in person, you can figure out who lives near camp by looking for their footprints and scat (poop).

tube-shaped scat; the size can indicate the size of the animal.

- **Cat family:** Water drop–shaped scat
- **Weasel family:** Wide thread shaped scat
- **Rabbits:** Tiny and round scat
- **Deer:** Pill-shaped scat
- **Rodents:** Long and thin small scat
- **Bats:** Bat scat is called guano and is usually small, dry, oval pellets. Guano collects under roost sites (where they sleep during the day), so you often see bat guano in small piles.
- **Birds:** There are as many different kinds of bird droppings as there are birds, but usually their droppings look like colored paint blotches because they have fallen from a long way to get to the ground. Most are pasty and white, but some are different. Bird droppings will be more three-dimensional if they are left on branches or by a bird that was on the ground at the time. If you find a lot of droppings under a tree, it might mean that the birds have nests in the tree, like to roost there, or the tree provides something they like to eat.
- **Birds of prey:** Owls, eagles, and hawks leave pellets, which are the undigested bones and hair they spit up. Pellets are not scat and are mostly round or oval shaped. Don't handle them unless they have been

Scat Search *(ages 6 and up)*

All animals leave droppings because they all have to eat and then get rid of their waste. Scientists call these droppings "scat." Bears, mice, snakes, lizards, frogs, and ladybugs all leave scat behind. Scat is one of the most important signs to look for when tracking animals. For scientists, an animal's scat can reveal the type of animal, what it's eaten, where it spends most of its time, and if it is sick or healthy. Different kinds of animals leave different kinds of scat, and knowing how to tell which is which can help you figure out what kinds of animals live nearby.

- **Foxes and coyotes:** The scat of many wild carnivores will be thick with the fur of the animals they've eaten.
- **Dogs, raccoons, skunks, opossums, wolverines, and bears:** All have thick

Psst . . . Kids! While searching for scat, never touch it with your bare hands. If you wish to take it apart to exam it more, use a stick. By the way, did you know that scat is also a word for improvisational singing in jazz using nonsense syllables? (Scat is a fun **homophone**: a word that is pronounced the same as another word but has a different meaning and may differ in spelling. Can you think of more?)

this dirt has been through their bodies, it is virtually the same as any other dirt.

dry-heat sterilized for several hours to remove bacteria and viruses. Once dry, however, you can dissect them to reveal the bones of prey.

- **Earthworms:** Invertebrates leave droppings too, usually very small ones. Earthworms dig tunnels in the ground by eating dirt. They often leave small, neat piles of smooth dirt on the ground. Though

Animal Track Search

With a little detective work, you can discover animal tracks. Look in soft dirt, mud, or snow to find indentations of animal paw prints. You might be surprised to find out how many kinds of critters live nearby. In some cases you can follow the tracks and learn more about an animal's movements and behaviors.

You can find more information about common animal tracks on the US Geological Survey (USGS) website or buy a track guidebook. Use your NATURE JOURNAL or be a

PHOTOJOURNALIST to record your findings!

Supplies: 2 rocks or sturdy sticks, a resonant tree or branch

Learn a little about woodpecker drumming. Woodpeckers do not have vocal cords, so they use drumming to communicate. They choose a resonant object to drum on, often a hollow log or tree. Woodpeckers drum for two main reasons: To say "This territory is mine!" and to attract a mate. (They also use their strong beaks to search tree trunks and branches for wood-boring beetles and other food, as well as to hollow out nests,

Call a Woodpecker

A telephone won't do it, but a woodpecker might answer your call made by knocking rocks or sticks against a resonate tree! The key is to call the right number, which in woodpecker means playing the right rhythm. Get ready for some tree drumming!

WHY WOODPECKERS DON'T GET HEADACHES

A human obviously could not drum the way a woodpecker does without serious head injuries. But woodpeckers have special characteristics that allow them to peck quickly and repeatedly on hard objects, namely thick skulls, strong neck muscles, and thick, straight bills. In more suburban settings, they will even drum on house siding, utility poles, rain gutters, trash-cans, and chimneys.

Did You Know?

Wonderful Woodpecker Facts

- A woodpecker can peck twenty times per second. It produces around 11,000 pecks per day.
- Woodpeckers have special feathers that look like bristles on their nostrils that prevent them from inhaling wood particles.
- Woodpeckers have zygodactil (zahy-guh-DAK-til) feet: four toes, with two facing forward and two backward. This arrangement ensures a strong grip to branches and is why woodpeckers can stand for long periods on the sides of trees. Woodpeckers also have a pair of centrally located feathers that provide stability and keep them in the upright position while standing on the trees.
- Woodpeckers have very long, sometime barbed tongues designed to capture prey hidden inside trees.
- Woodpeckers have a unique flying pattern: Three wing flaps are followed by gliding. This pattern repeats all the time during flight.
- Woodpeckers are monogamous, meaning a pair mates for a lifetime. Both males and females prepare the nest. The female lays usually two to five eggs that hatch after eleven to fourteen days. One month after hatching, young woodpeckers are ready to leave the nest.
- Probably the most well-known woodpecker is the cartoon bird Woody Woodpecker, created by Walter Lanz and artist Ben "Bugs" Hardaway in 1940. Woody has a distinctive, repetitive laugh that plays on a woodpecker's drumming.

but the pecking is different, usually shorter in duration.) Each woodpecker species has its own pattern of drumming with its own tempo, length, and rhythm. During breeding season, usually late April and May, you will generally hear more woodpeckers drumming.

Get your drumming supplies and drum. Find two sturdy sticks or two rocks that you can hold comfortably one in each hand. Experiment by hitting your "drumsticks" against different trees, branches, or logs until you find one that helps the sound travel farther. It helps if the branch or log is fairly dry. Try trunks with and without bark.

Listen for woodpecker drumming to imitate. If you don't hear any woodpeckers, try a rhythm anyway. Or ask a naturalist what kind of woodpeckers live in the area and what their drumming sounds like (or look it up yourself).

Drum, be still, and listen. Relax your arms and use your wrists to hammer out the rhythm you heard. Pause and listen. If you don't hear the woodpecker call back, try again. Stop and listen each time. If a woodpecker answers, drum again. Listen and watch. The woodpecker might fly closer to you to take a better look at this rival woodpecker or possible mate in its territory.

Catch a Lizard *(ages 9 and up)*

You don't have to catch a lizard to enjoy watching it dart across your path or hang out doing push-ups on a warm rock. (Being cold-blooded, they need that sunshine to heat their blood and get moving.) But if you do want to catch a lizard, all you need is a stick, a sturdy blade of grass (or dental floss), a slipknot, and a firm but caring hand (for this reason, this activity is not recommended for children under 8 or 9 years old). Biologists often use this method to catch lizards and study them.

Supplies:

- A long, thin stick, 2–3 feet long, preferably with a little flexibility
- A strong, long stem of grass or waxed dental floss 2–3 feet long

Best Time. Early- or midmorning is one of the best times to catch a lizard, when the sun pulls them out of hiding but before they've had a chance to really warm up and are still moving slowly. Don't harm or traumatize the lizard. The idea is to appreciate and learn about these amazing creatures by touching them and observing them up close. Never hold a lizard by a leg or by the tail. And never squeeze one too tightly.

Make a slipknot in your grass or floss. It might help to chew the tip a little and moisten it with your spit. Make your slipknot by forming a loop at one end of the grass and pinch where the grass overlaps with your thumb and forefinger. With your other hand, reach through that loop and pull a new loop of grass through the first loop. Keep pulling that new loop until it is tightened. (See page 105 for more on tying knots.)

Attach the grass to the stick. Tie the grass to the thinner end of your stick so that the loop hangs between 4 and 6 inches from the end of the stick.

Approach the lizard slowly from the front or side. Oddly, this tends to work better if the lizard can see you. The lizard will focus on your approach instead of on the noose. Only come close enough to reach the lizard with your noose. Sudden movements will cause the lizard to run away and hide.

Gently fit the noose around the lizard's head. The lizard's own weight should tighten the slipknot as it moves, preventing it from escaping. Some species and individuals react quickly to the noose; others will remain motionless even as the noose bumps into them several times.

Carefully remove the noose. Grasp the lizard gently but firmly by the back, not the tail, limbs, or head. Pull the noose off in short, gentle motions, or simply break the grass.

Gently hold and observe the lizard. You'll find that most lizards respond to the warmth of your hands and your slow movements by relaxing. Some may not want to leave your hand when you're ready to let them go! Be a PHOTOJOURNALIST and capture your lizard.

Let your lizard go. Don't hold on to your lizard for more than 10 minutes if you don't have a suitable home for it. Gently release your lizard at ground level by encouraging it to run off your hand onto a rock or the ground where you found it. Describe the animal and the event in your NATURE JOURNAL.

Did You Know?

The Lowdown on Lizards!

Lizards first appeared on Earth over 200 million years ago. There are over 4,600 lizard species, with new types still being discovered. Many lizards have extremely good color vision and smell with their tongues. They don't have earflaps like mammals do. Instead, they have ear openings to catch sound, and their eardrums are just below the surface of their skin. Lizards can't hear as well as people, but their hearing is better than that of snakes. When young lizards grow, their scaly skin doesn't. That's why they have to shed or molt old skin, usually in large flakes. (The alligator lizard sheds its skin in one piece like a snake.) Male lizards do push-ups to try to attract a female's attention.

The largest lizard in the world is the Komodo dragon, which can grow up to 10 feet long and weigh 150 pounds. This giant reptile can only be found on a few Indonesian islands, including Komodo. The smallest lizards in the world are also island lizards: the Jaragua lizard, a dwarf gecko found in the Dominican Republic, and tiny leaf chameleons from Madagascar. The smallest measures 0.064 inch (15 mm) from the tip of the snout to the base of the tail.

Catch a Crawdad *(ages 9 and up)*

Camping near a lake? Also known as crayfish, crawdads are amazing-looking creatures. With their hard shells (exoskeletons), they still resemble their prehistoric ancestors. Even without a fishing pole, you can catch and release crawdads so you won't hurt the creatures but can have a better look at them.

Supplies:

- String
- Stick
- Bait: bacon, salami, pepperoni, or other fatty meat
- Bucket or pot

Photo by David Rolf

Find a fairly long, sturdy stick and tie your string to the end of it. Tie some bait directly to the string at the other end. Look for crawdads along the shore of a lake, stream, or river. They like to hang out underneath rocks along the edge of the water. Dangle the bait in the water, allowing it to sink to the bottom near the edge of the rocks or bank, and wait for a crawdad to find the bait. When the crawdad pinches the bait, pull it out of the water at a steady, moderate speed and dangle the crawdad over a bucket. When the crawdad realizes it is hanging in the air, it will let go and fall into the bucket. The safest way to hold a crawdad is to place your thumb and fingers pointing forward on the main part of the shell just behind the claws so it can't pinch you.

Be a Dew Predictor

Dew be or not dew be? Be Nostradamus of the campground! Amaze your family with your ability to predict if there will be dew in the morning.

First, you need to understand what dew is. Dew forms in the early morning or late evening, but only under certain conditions and not on everything. On a warm day, water evaporates from the warm ground into the air. When it does this, it is turning from a liquid into a gas called "water vapor." When evening comes, the warm ground continues to radiate heat into the air. As the ground begins to cool, the air will not be able to hold all the moisture. At a certain point—a temperature called the "dew point"—water vapor in the air will turn back to liquid faster than the water is evaporating (condensation). When this happens, dew forms.

Here's what to look for: If a warm, clear day is followed by a cool, clear evening, dew will likely form. It's important that the evening is clear for dew formation, because cloudy nights hold heat closer to the ground. If the evening is cloudy, the clouds reflect heat back to the ground. When this happens, the ground doesn't cool off enough for dew to form.

Where to find dew. Dew only appears on surfaces that aren't warmed by the heat radiated from the ground. That's why you mainly see dew on things like grass, leaves, and spiderwebs, surfaces that are nice and cool. The plants in a flowerbed keep the ground warm enough to prevent dew. So you can even predict where dew will form: nowhere where it's warm!

Just DEW it!

Other Searches

You can search for so many wonderful things in nature. If you see ladybugs on the trail, look for more. Here are a few other things to search for in the outdoors.

Mushrooms. You can find a wide variety of shapes and colors in fungi. Never eat them, and if you handle them, be sure to wash your hands thoroughly.

Did You Know?

A Memo on Mushrooms

A few fun facts on this fascinating fungus: Another word for a mushroom is toadstool. Because mushrooms are fungi, they do not require sunlight to create energy for themselves. Mushrooms are 90 percent water. Over thirty species of mushrooms actually glow in the dark!

Wildflowers. Don't pick them, but look for different varieties and colors. Does the plant need lots of water or sunlight? Look at the conditions where it is growing.

Different trees. How many different trees grow in your area? What are the characteristics of each? How do they live together?

Butterflies and moths. It is always a treat to see an intricately patterned butterfly drying its wings or fluttering about. Keep your eyes open for more!

Measuring Water Depth

How deep is that creek? You can make your own simple measuring device and compare how deep the creek is in different places. This is really handy when you have to cross a larger stream!

Supplies: A long stick and a pencil or pocket-knife (optional)

Find a fairly long, sturdy stick. This will become your ruler. Stick it in the water as far as it can go. See how far the water comes up the stick, and estimate the depth. Was it as deep as you estimated? Mark the stick to compare that depth to other areas of water.

Fossils. Research before your trip if fossils are likely to exist where you are exploring. If they are, look in rocks and around creekbeds. Ancient seashells generally are the most common fossil to find.

Exploring with Measurement

Measuring things—distance, volume, temperature, speed—is a major part of being a scientist. Here are some fun ways to explore nature with measurements.

How Old Is That Tree?

See that fallen tree on the ground? How old do you think it was when it fell? You can figure that out by counting its rings.

Each year, trees don't just grow upwards; their trunks also get fatter. Looking at a cross

Tidbits about Trees

- Trees are very complex organisms. A tree trunk is actually the plant's stem. The stem supports the tree, stores and moves nutrients and water up and down and out to branches and leaves, and holds the leaves or needles so they can soak up the sunlight. Its bark protects the stem.
- Trees grow tall because they are competing with other trees for sunlight, which they need to survive. Trees that are not tall enough are called shrubs.
- Trees can live for thousands of years.
- The tallest species of trees in the world is the coast redwood, with some measuring 328 feet in height.
- The giant sequoia is not only tall but also wide, its shallow roots spreading great distances. Because of this, some believe that the giant sequoia is the largest living organism on Earth.
- Trees produce oxygen and reduce the amount of carbon dioxide in our atmosphere.

section of the trunk, you can see the rings. Trees usually grow best in spring, when it's wet, making a light-colored ring. In summer, or dry season, trees don't grow as much, making a dark-colored ring. **1 light-colored ring + 1 dark-colored ring = 1 year.** This is called a *growth ring.*

Tell the age of the tree when it fell by counting the rings. Each pair of light and dark rings is one year of life. This takes some patience for older, bigger trees, so you can also estimate by counting a number of rings, say ten. Measure that section with a marked stick or measuring tape. How many stick lengths does it take to reach the center of the trunk? Count those. Now multiply that number by 10 to get an approximate age of the tree. This will be an estimate, because the thickness of tree rings varies depending on how good or bad the environment and weather was for the tree each year.

Variations

- Look for rings that are wider or thinner than others. The wider rings mark years when the amount of rain and temperature were good for the tree. In this way you are studying the history of the local climate. Scientists who do this are called paleoclimatologists (pail-ee-oh-cly-muh-TALL-oh-jists). They study climate change.

- Look for strange marks, like scars or unusual patterns. Scars can be left by insects or disease. A forest fire can leave burn marks.

Measuring Temperature with Crickets

If you hear crickets at night, they can help you tell the temperature. The frequentness of their chirps depends on the temperature. Determine the temperature (in Fahrenheit degrees) by adding 37 to the number of chirps produced in 15 seconds. The higher the temperature, the more frequent the chirps.

Did You Know?

Decoding Cricket Song

Only male crickets make song. They have comblike structures on their wings that produce a chirping sound when they rub them together. They sing mostly to attract females but sometimes to ward off other male crickets. There are over 900 species around the world, and in some places, crickets are a symbol of good luck.

Make Your Own Compass

Want to know if you are heading north, east, south, or west and don't have a compass with you? Never fear! You can measure direction by making your own compass out of a stick in the ground, a few small rocks, and a little sunlight. Try this in camp too.

Find a stick and plant it in a flat spot of relatively clear ground so it goes straight up and down. The stick should be tall enough to cast a good shadow. Place a rock where the stick's shadow ends. Check the stick again in about 20 minutes. (The more time, the more accurate the direction will be.) Again place a rock where the stick's shadow ends. (You can tell if it is before or after noon. Did the shadow get longer? If yes, then it is afternoon. If no, it is still before noon.) Draw a line between the two marks you have made on the ground, or connect them with another nice, straight stick. You have just made your east-west line. The first mark you made will be west; the second mark will be east. Draw another line bisecting the line you just drew on the ground, or use a stick so that it looks like a big plus sign. That line points north and south.

Make a Sundial

Measure time and build a sundial the way humans did it before the invention of the clock. To get started, you need a good place in the sun. A sundial is also called a shadow clock.

Supplies:

- A watch or other timepiece
- A timer with alarm (optional)
- A clear space on the ground, a table, or a flat piece of cardboard
- 13 rocks
- A stick
- Paper and pen or chalk

1. Find an area on the ground, about 2 by 3 feet, in full sunlight.

2. Pound a stick into the ground halfway across the space. It should be at least 7 or 8 inches high above the ground.

3. Mark the first hour. Place a stone on the ground at the end of the stick's shadow. With chalk, write the time on the stone, trace it in the dirt with a stick, or write it on

Did You Know?

Sunny Facts about Sundials

Humans first made sundials around 5,000 to 6,000 years ago in the great civilizations of the Middle East and North Africa, but the oldest sundials that still exist today date back to 1500 BC in ancient Egypt and Babylonia (Iraq today). However, it wasn't until the seventeenth century that they were designed on an accurate mathematical basis. Before the watch, people sometimes carried pocket sundials. The story goes that George Washington carried a pocket sundial in preference to the inaccurate watches available in his day. A sundial is actually a miniature Earth. The sun is so large compared to the Earth, and so far away, that the shadows on the dial are exactly the way the shadows fall on the whole Earth.

The tallest sundial in the world is actually a super skyscraper, the Taipei 101 in Taiwan. Next to the 1,670-foot building is the circular Clock Park, which doubles as the face of a giant sundial. The tower itself casts the shadow to mark afternoon hours for the building's occupants.

a piece of paper and put it under the stone so it won't blow away.

4. If using a timer, set it to go off every hour; go do other stuff in the meantime.

5. One hour later, place a stone on the ground at the end of the stick's shadow. Mark the time.

6. Repeat this every hour that you are in camp. You will mark off thirteen hours. For example, if you start with 6 a.m., you will finish with 6 p.m. If you are off hiking or swimming, place rocks for the missing hours where you think they might go. You can check them if you are in camp at those times by comparing the time your sundial indicates to the actual time. Make adjustments if necessary.

7. The next day, you'll only need to look at the shadow on your sundial to tell the time.

Exploring at Night

From twilight into the darkness of night, there is so much to explore. As the sun starts to set, check out the world around you by trying one of these activities. Record the moments in your NATURE JOURNAL and bring your camera along to be a PHOTOJOURNALIST.

Take In the Sunset

Find a place where you can take in the sunset. What colors do you see in the sky? How do they change and how quickly? During sunset, sunlight just above the horizon is traveling through the atmosphere to reach your eyes. This eliminates a lot of the light and gives the sun its red color.

Animals at Twilight: Crepuscular, Diurnal, or Nocturnal?

- Animals that are primarily active at twilight are called **crepuscular** (crep-US-kue-lar). One example is a rabbit.

- Animals mostly active during the day are called **diurnal** (dye-ER-nul). Hawks are diurnal.
- Animals that are mostly active at night are called **nocturnal** (nok-TER-nul). Owls are nocturnal.

Take a guess with your family. What animals are crepuscular, diurnal, or nocturnal? Some are more than one! If you're not sure, write down your guesses in your NATURE JOURNAL and check your answers when you get home.

Getting the Knack of Nocturnal Animals
You already know that humans are by nature diurnal, active by day. That makes night critters seem pretty mysterious to us daytime dwellers. Nocturnal animals often sleep during the day in a burrow or den or other hidden place. Some have special features that allow them to operate well at night, especially their eyes. There are lots of books at your school and public library and websites that can acquaint

Why Are Some Animals Nocturnal?
There are many reasons. Some animals operate at night because there is less competition for food, water, and space. Others are awake at night to escape predators that would hunt them during the day. Many desert animals are nocturnal in order to escape extreme daytime heat.

Special Adaptations: Nocturnal animals have special adaptations that help them survive in the dark. Owls, lemurs, and cats have specialized eyes to see well in the dark. Bats use echolocation. Many crepuscular and nocturnal animals, like rabbits, have good hearing.

you with the animals of the night and the sounds they make. But while camping, you can explore them in the flesh with these activities.

Nocturnal Noise
Listen! The sounds nocturnal animals make can be beautiful, especially if you know what wonderful animal is making each sound and why. Take the rhythmic song of crickets or the hollow hooting of an owl.

Try to make out the sounds of specific animals and identify them. Ask another member of your family to identify them. Make up your own animals! Just be respectful; if you have campers who are afraid of the dark, try not to make them scary. With campers who like spooky tales, go for it!

Grab your headlamp and a pencil and try to describe each sound in your NATURE JOURNAL.

Search for Nocturnal Aquatic Animals

Suspend a waterproof flashlight in a pond or lake, and with a bucket or container, catch water creatures attracted to the light. Scoop up some water in the dark. Compare what animals were in the illuminated water versus the dark water. Pour or immerse them carefully back into their habitat.

Toad & Frog Conversation

If you are near water, chances are there are toads and frogs nearby too. Listen for toad and frog calls. There are as many different frog calls as there are species of frogs. Try to imitate each sound you hear. How many toads or frogs do you think are making those sounds?

A Light Attraction

Turn on a lantern or your flashlight, leave it in one place for a while, and watch the insects gather around it. What insects do you see? Why do you think they are attracted to the light? Share and discuss this with your family.

The Night Sky

Before going into your tent for the night, take a few minutes after dark with your family to look up. Keep looking! What do you see? Ask one another what you see.

The sky above us is full of amazing things that incite wonder: the stars, the moon, the planets, and the vastness of it all. Observe the sky several evenings in a row and you'll notice that the sky looks different each night than it did the night before. The moon may appear to be getting larger or smaller. The stars may seem brighter and more noticeable (or dimmer and harder to see). The sky itself may seem brighter or darker. Do you wonder why?

Finding Constellations

Constellations (con-stell-AY-shuns) are groupings of stars that form easily recognized and remembered patterns, such as Orion, with his belt of three stars in a row, and the Big Dipper, shaped like a cup with a handle.

Finding the North Star

It's easy to find the North Star (also known as Polaris) in the sky as long as you can see the Big Dipper. Draw a line with your eye from the bottom star of the Big Dipper's bowl farthest from the handle to the star at the top of the bowl farthest from the handle. See that distance? Count out about five of those in a straight line from the line you just made. The star you reach is the North Star. It is the end of the handle of the Little Dipper. Long before GPS units, people used the North Star to tell direction. If you stand facing the North Star, you're facing the direction north. But this only works in the Northern Hemisphere. South of the equator, the North Star is below the horizon.

Did You Know?

The Big Dipper is actually an asterism (AS-tuh-riz-uhm), not a constellation, because it is only part of the constellation Ursa Major (the Big Bear). Actually, the stars in the majority of all constellations do not "belong together." Usually they are at greatly varying distances from Earth and just happen to lie more or less in the same line of sight as seen from our solar system. Orion's stars lie at distances ranging from 243 to 1,360 light years from us!

What is a light year? It is a unit of astronomical distance equivalent to the distance that light travels in one year, which is 9.4607×10^{12} km (nearly 6 trillion miles)!

But in a few cases, the stars of a constellation are actually associated; most of the bright stars of the Big Dipper travel together and form what astronomers call an open cluster.

Phases of the Moon

There are eight phases of the moon. What phase is the moon in now? Create your own Phases of the Moon Chart and find out!

On a piece of paper, draw two rows with four boxes in each, leaving enough room for a picture of the moon, a title, and an explanation. Or you can draw the phases in a circle or whatever way you like.

Start with the new moon, followed by the waxing crescent, etc., in order. Draw a picture of each moon, label it, and add explanations like these:

- New moon: This is the beginning of the moon phases, when the moon is nearly invisible.

- Waxing crescent: This is the sliver of a crescent when the moon begins to increase in size.

- First quarter: At this point, the moon is at its first 90-degree angle.

- Waxing gibbous: The moon is illuminated to a 135-degree angle.

- Full moon: The entire moon is lit up by the sun, so you can see the whole disc.

- Waxing gibbous: The illumination of the moon starts to shrink again.

- Last quarter: The moon is at its second 90-degree angle.

- Waning crescent: This is the last phase of the moon.

Add any other designs or illustrations, borders, or colors you want around your chart. Take a look at the moon each night you are camping, and mark the date on your chart. (You can also do this at home.) You are officially an astronomer!

Other Celestial Bodies

What else can you see in the night sky? Look for planets, bright stars, satellites, and meteor showers (or shooting stars). First, just recline and look around the sky. If you can't identify planets and stars or locate satellites (they look like stars moving at a steady pace in a straight line in the sky), you can use a planet finder app on a smartphone to help you.

Meteor Showers

Whenever a small space particle (meteoroid) enters the Earth's atmosphere, it generates a flash of light called a meteor, or "shooting star." Meteor showers occur

WANT TO SEE THE INTERNATIONAL SPACE STATION?

The third brightest object in the sky, the space station is easy to see if you know when to look up. You can find the location of the Space Station in the sky above you at spotthestation.nasa.gov.

when a comet comes close to the sun during its orbit and produces debris (meteoroids) that spread around the comet's orbit. Because these comets move in a steady orbit, some meteor showers occur at the same time every year. One example is the Perseid meteor shower, one of the brighter meteor showers of the year, which takes place every year between July 17 and August 24, peaking around August 9–13. It is made of tiny space debris from Comet Swift-Tuttle. The Perseids are named for the constellation Perseus, since the shower lies in the same direction as that constellation, found in the northeastern part of the sky. You can find a calendar of meteor showers in an almanac or online at almanac.com.

CHAPTER 5

PLAYING IN THE LANDSCAPE

Inventions, experiments, and amusements abound in nature. This chapter suggests ways to play in nature that will enhance your outdoor experience. Some are old and familiar, like skipping rocks, building forts, and whittling, and perhaps some will be new to your family, like making your own nest or rainbow. While playing in the landscape, you might be doing science, building stuff, or learning essential camping and survival skills. Not a bad way to have fun. It is proven that play is good for everyone, so go out and play in the landscape!

> *Look! A trickle of water running through some dirt! I'd say our afternoon just got booked solid!*
>
> —Bill Watterson *(Calvin & Hobbes)*

Rocks Rock!

Rocks can provide hours of entertainment! As you read in the previous chapter, you can identify and collect them. You can also paint them, sort them, pretend with them, break them apart, crush them, throw them at various targets (nonliving of course), pile them into sculptures, or arrange them into frescos, pathways, labyrinths, and more. If you need markers for

a board game or chips for poker, small rocks will do the trick!

Here are some rockin' fun activities you can do with rocks.

Tracing Shapes with Rocks *(ages 2 and up)*

With a stick and rocks, create pictures of any kind on the ground.

Supplies: Rocks and a stick (or optional chalk)

You can do this fun activity with a partner or by yourself. Begin by drawing—or have your partner draw—simple shapes with a stick on the ground or on the picnic table with a piece of chalk. Hunt around to find lots of rocks. You can use twigs, leaves, or other stuff too. Place the rocks along the drawn lines. It's that simple, but the results can be very beautiful.

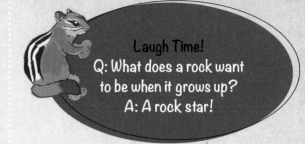

Laugh Time!
Q: What does a rock want to be when it grows up?
A: A rock star!

Make the shapes more complicated as you go. You can trace letters and numbers too, objects or animals.

Variation

Make up a story about the pictures and shapes that you're tracing, and share it with a fellow camper or write it in your NATURE JOURNAL.

Rock Shop *(ages 3–9)*

Come and buy your rocks here! Special gems, gold within, mystery rocks! Set up your own store full of rock displays, and invite your friends and family to come shopping!

Supplies:

- Rocks (pinecones, leaves, and sticks are optional)
- Containers, plates or boxes (optional)

1. Collect a number of interesting looking rocks of different sizes and colors.
2. Sort the rocks and set them up on a boulder, stump, log, or your picnic table.
3. You can use repurposed boxes, containers, or plates from your camping kitchen for display cases and your cashbox.
4. Small pebbles or leaves can be your money. Provide some "money" to other campers (or ask them to collect their own) and invite them to your Rock Shop to buy your rocks. You decide the price!

Variation

Pretend that the rocks have magic or useful properties. (**Examples:** This one held in your palm relaxes you; this one when mixed in tea with feathers can make you fly; this one is a fortune-telling rock—stare at it and see the future, etc.)

Skipping Stones

Skipping stones on water has long been a beloved outdoor activity. Kids can ask grandparents if they remember skipping stones when they were young; chances are they have fond memories of this awesome natural pastime. If you have never skipped stones before, be patient! It can take awhile to develop a throw that will get you multiple skips on the water, even if you already know how to throw a baseball or football.

Here are some tips to help you get some radical skips:

Choosing your water. The best water is flat—the surface of a lake or river without wind or whitewater. If you do try to skip stones on rough water, you'll need to adapt your technique to using a slightly heavier stone, which is more likely to plow through a wave and maintain a steady course. In general, though, heavier stones are harder to wield.

Choosing your stones. The ideal rock is skinny, flat and round, about the size of your palm, just heavy enough to be immune to breezes and turbulence, but still light enough to be thrown with accuracy. Usually finding the "perfect" skipping stone is a treasure in itself! Collect a bunch of rocks as close to this ideal shape as possible. But any palm-sized or smaller rock with at least one flat size can be skipped a bit. It's great to start with a pile so you can skip one after the other before searching for more stones.

Holding the stone. Place your index finger against the edge of the rock. Place the stone in the crook of your index finger, resting on the side of your middle finger on the bottom, with

Psst . . . Kids! Throw your stone as fast as you can without losing form, but remember that angle and spin are more important than speed. And always make sure there is no one standing between you and the water before you throw.

your thumb on top of the rock to maintain control of it. This is just one way to hold the stone; what matters, ultimately, is that you can send the stone spinning in a straight line with the flat end almost parallel to the water.

The stance. Face the water sideways, with your feet shoulder-width apart. Stand with your non-dominant side closer to the water's edge, your shoulder turned toward the water. Squat down close to the water so that when you throw, your rock will be close to parallel with the surface of the water. Scientists have found that the ideal angle between the stone and the water is 20 degrees. Any less than that, and the friction slows it down; any more than that, and the stone cuts the water and sinks. (It's so cool that scientists have studied this!)

The throw. Bend your wrist all the way back and then snap it forward to flick the rock against the surface of the water. Don't think of it as throwing an overhand Frisbee but as throwing an underhand softball or cracking a whip sideways. The important thing is that you carefully bend your wrist all the way back to generate some power and

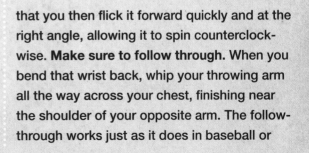

that you then flick it forward quickly and at the right angle, allowing it to spin counterclockwise. **Make sure to follow through.** When you bend that wrist back, whip your throwing arm all the way across your chest, finishing near the shoulder of your opposite arm. The follow-through works just as it does in baseball or tennis; the full motion will get you the longest, most powerful throw.

Get your legs into it. After you feel like you have a strong sense of how to get the speed, spin, and angle that you're going for with your hands and arms, work on getting your legs into it so that you can generate even more power and master your rhythm and technique. Bend down at least 6 inches, and get some bend in your knees.

Keep practicing. If the stone bounces off the water and goes high in the air, you're probably throwing it down too close to yourself. Try throwing it so the first skip is farther away from you. The force of the water pushes the rock up, and with too much force, it goes too far up, comes down at a sharp angle, and sinks. If you throw it too far, though, the stone will "surf" across the surface of the water (rather than skip); the friction will slow the rock's momentum and cause it to sink. You can also practice skipping stones of different sizes and weights. You may find that you prefer a smaller, lighter stone or a larger, heavier stone.

Did You Know?
The Guinness World Record for skipping stones is sixty-five skips in one throw (set by Maxwell Steiner in 2014 at Riverfront Park, Franklin, Pennsylvania). Epic! You can see the skip on YouTube.

Rock a Bull's-Eye *(ages 8 and up)*
Get your throwing arm ready, and try to hit the target!

Supplies: Rocks and safe natural targets

Oh, yeah, it's target practice time! The key for this game is making absolutely sure no human or animal, or car or building or tent, could accidentally get hit with a rock. Okay? Now the fun begins. Pick a target or multiple targets. A good one is the end of a fallen tree or log. It has a natural bull's-eye because of the age rings inside the wood. Boulders or the sides of trees work. So do piles of rocks or low-hanging branches. Gather your supply of throwing rocks. You might try some of varying weights to see what works best. Choose a spot to throw from, marking the spot. Everyone stays behind the line and take turns trying to hit the targets.

Variations

- Make a target gallery in which you have a certain amount of time to try to hit several different targets.
- By a lake? Float driftwood out into the water and try to hit it.

Making a Labyrinth *(ages 8 and up, but even younger kids can help)*
In a clear space, align rocks to create the curving pathways of a maze or labyrinth (LAB-uh-rinth) and invite others to walk it! What's the difference? A **maze** offers choices of more than one path at intersections. Some paths may dead-end. A **labyrinth** provides one winding path toward the center.

Supplies:

- Rocks
- Sticks and other woodland debris (optional)
- Shrine offerings, such as trinkets, toys, jewelry, crafts (optional)

Find or clear an area of dirt or grass. Design the labyrinth. You can draw it on a piece of paper first, use a variation of the pattern shown here, or just wing it. You can create choices in the path (maze), different branches to walk, or just one coil-like path (labyrinth). Just remember that the path eventually goes to the center. Collect rocks or other building materials. You'll need to collect a lot of rocks to mark the outside circle and all the pathways. Short on rocks? You can use branches, logs, sticks, leaves, pinecones, whatever

THE LOWDOWN ON LABYRINTHS

For thousands of years, human beings have created labyrinths for decoration, art, and myth. A labyrinth is a spiral path that folds back on itself and around in different directions leading to a central point. Labyrinths have long been used as creative and spiritual tools, often as paths for meditation. Some people say if you have a problem, you can use a labyrinth to help solve it or, walking a labyrinth, you can find inspiration.

Stone labyrinth on Blå Jungfrun (Blue Virgin) Island, Sweden   *Photo by Mingusrude*

works for you. Make the heart of the labyrinth. The center can be a clear place to sit and contemplate or can contain a shrine of some sort. You decide.

Creating your labyrinth can be a rewarding solitary activity, but it is also a great group activity, because it can take a long time to place all the rocks and complete it. Consider building it in a clearing a little distance from the general population or away from any popular hiking paths. That way, if it takes you several days to build your labyrinth, it is less likely to be disturbed in the process.

Walking the Labyrinth *(all ages)*

Invite your family and other campers to walk your labyrinth. For a meditative or spiritual journey, you might offer them these instructions:

1. **Stand in front of the entrance to the labyrinth and state your intention as clearly as possible.** For example: "I want a solution to my problem with . . . " (It could be anything that is troubling you.) or "I want inspiration to . . ." Are you being spiritual, reflective, mindful, playful, creative, or something else?

2. **Center yourself by taking a couple of deep breaths and begin your walk.** Your pace can be fast or slow. If you are very upset, walking in quickly allows the emotions to dissipate more easily. Or you might try walking at a slow pace to slow the mind.

3. **Continue to walk.** Keep your mind quiet, and still pestering thoughts each time they arise. Concentrate on the placement of one foot before the other and rhythmic, gentle, and regular breathing. If you're

problem solving, walk as if you don't have any problems at all; let it all go. Surrender to the activity of attentive walking. This allows your body to process your wish for a solution. All you have to do is to let it incubate and not interfere. Let go of any expectations.

4. **Pause on reaching the center.** Stop in the center for a while; sit or lie down if you feel like it, and meditate or reflect. It feels good to have all the time you need. If there is a shrine, you can take something from it as an anonymous gift of gratitude. You may want to leave a treasure for someone else. It could be a feather, a cool stick, a trinket or coin, something you have made or even a written message.

5. **When you are ready, just walk out.** Accept the insights and gifts you may have received. Offer your thanks for what you have learned. Gratitude is always fruitful!

Nature Shrine *(ages 3 and up)*

Create your own special shrine for your family. If anyone is celebrating a birthday, it can become a birthday shrine. Or simply fill it with beautiful or interesting things and feel your gratitude for nature.

Supplies: Found natural and other objects

Find a secret or sacred place near camp that won't be disturbed, and clear a space. Start collecting cool-looking bits of nature: moss, interesting-shaped wood, colorful rocks, feathers, as well as found items (a horseshoe or rusty can). Organize them into a work of art, piling rocks or making pictures or patterns out of the objects however you want. If there are

Supplies: Sticks, leaves, or pinecones

Player finds a stick or the like to be their boat. Decide on a starting point and a finish line. The start could be a bridge or near a rock on the riverbank. The finish line can also be marked by something along the river, but it should be very clear. On your mark, get set . . . on "go," put your boat on or throw it out into the water. Watch the boats move with the

old burnt-out stumps around, you can use the charcoaled wood to add a message on the rocks.

Stick with Sticks

Think rafts, log cabins, fences, and tepees! Sticks are an ideal building material to play with and invent with while you are hanging out in nature. Try out some of these pastimes with sticks, or make up some of your own.

Stick Boat Races *(ages 4 and up)*

Hiking by a river or stream? Use leaves, sticks, pinecones, or any natural object you think might float to boat race.

current. The winner is the first to pass the finish line.

Variations

- Be a water scientist. Time your stick to test the current or speed of the water flow, which is caused by gravity. Try this several times, logging it in your NATURE JOURNAL, and figure out the average to get an accurate measure. Experiment with the speed of other natural objects, like leaves and pinecones.
- Locate an eddy at the side of the river or creek. In an eddy, the stick will not move down the river; in fact, it might just turn in circles. An eddy is a circular movement of water counter to a main current, causing a small whirlpool. These are important for kayakers and canoers. They use eddies as landing spots if they want to stop for a while.
- Drop a stick down a waterfall and see if you can follow its journey with your eyes on its quick ride down.
- Be a PHOTOJOURNALIST and film the race, narrating it like a sports announcer.
- **Sailboat Regatta.** Build a boat that can stay afloat! Make sailboats using only natural objects or repurposed materials from your camping kitchen. Give it a sail made of a leaf or paper, use a stick for a mast, put it on water in a pot or basin or in the lake with you, and blow. Race your sailboats in your own regatta!

Build a Dam *(ages 4 and up)*

Can you build a structure that stops a river from flowing and controls how much water passes through? How about out of sticks and rocks?

Supplies:

- Rocks and sticks
- Bucket of water
- Hand shovel or pail (optional)

> Psst...Kids! The deeper the water, the greater the water pressure, so the bottom of your dam will need to support more pressure than the top of your dam. If you built your dam in a triangular shape, the bottom will be wider and will be able to support more pressure.

Dig a miniature "river" on the ground or on the beach. Choose a spot somewhere along the river to build your dam. Use sticks and small rocks to construct a dam that will let only a little bit of water come through, but not too much. Test your dam by pouring water from a bucket down the river path. Experiment with different designs.

Make a Nest *(ages 5 and up)*

Birds can do it. Can you build a nest that could hold a clutch of eggs and withstand the wind?

Supplies:

- Woodland debris: branches, twigs, dead grass, and fallen leaves
- Rocks or pinecones
- A tree with a low fork

Look for materials on the woodland floor that you could use—for example, dried grasses, twigs, sticks, and lichen. Now find a low fork in a tree and build your nest. If you want to give yourself an extra challenge, try using just one hand—the bird only has its beak after all! If there are two of you, you could use one hand each and work together.

When you have finished, look for several small stones, cones, or other objects that could be your eggs. Place them in your nest to see if it will hold them. Then, with your eggs still in the nest, give the branch a little shake to see if your nest would stand up to the wind!

Build a Giant Nest *(ages 2 and up)*

Build a nest big enough for you!

Supplies: Woodland debris: branches, twigs, dead grass, and fallen leaves

Build your nest on the ground. Many birds lay their nests on the ground. Turkeys and pheasants, terns and sandpipers, wood ducks, and meadowlarks all nest on the ground. Shore birds such as gulls and puffins do this too!

Stack sticks in a circle, overlapping one another, to build the sides of the nest. Fill in the center with soft things like dead grass, feathers, and fallen leaves. Sit in it to test if it's comfy. If you were a baby bird, would you feel safe here?

Variations

- Build a giant stick ship or spaceship.
- How about a time machine? Suddenly you have arrived in Jurassic times! Or the

Ten Intriguing Facts about Nests

- A bird's nest is sturdy and secure enough to withstand the harshest winter, but a nest is not a home, like your house or tent. Birds use it just to hold their eggs and protect their young. When the babies are old enough to leave, the parents often abandon the nest.
- Birds know instinctively how to build nests. Birds raised in captivity can build one even if they've never seen one before.
- A nest has many layers, each with a specific purpose. Birds often use coarse twigs for the base. They lace together finer twigs and weeds and bark to create the bowl. For the lining, they use dry leaves, fine grasses, and other soft materials.
- City birds have learned to incorporate man-made items into their nests, such as paper, string, nails, pieces of wire, and fabric. They might even make their nest in an old tin can.
- Some birds line their nests with specific plants that keep away mites and other parasites that could harm their babies.
- Some birds include pieces of shed snakeskin in their nest lining to deter predators. Wouldn't want to bother a mama snake!
- Ducks and quail use their own down feathers to line their nests. Other birds collect feathers dropped by larger birds. Some fast-flying small birds will even strike big birds in flight in order to knock feathers loose.
- Female birds usually do all the construction, but in some species the male bird builds the foundation and leaves the detailed lining to the female. Some males build multiple "dummy" nests around the area to fool predators.
- Nests can vary from tiny to huge. Though the typical nest is shaped like a bowl, some nests look like hanging purses, haystacks in trees, balls of mud, and mounds on the ground. Hummingbirds build tiny thimble-size nests and line them with spiderwebs. Bald eagles build gigantic nests that can be 20 feet deep and weigh 2 tons!
- Many creatures, including wasps, mice, and alligators, build nests. But none are as intricately designed as a bird's nest.

time of cavemen and mastodons! Perhaps you're in a medieval forest!

- What else can you build?

Build a Den *(ages 2, with parental help, and up)*

Many animals, like squirrels, chipmunks, voles, beavers, foxes, bears, bobcats, and raccoons, dig or build burrows and dens to live in. Now it's your turn to build a woodland den for yourself! It's fun to play in, but this is also an outdoor survival skill: making emergency shelter.

Supplies: Woodland debris: fallen branches and twigs

To get started, find a sturdy, living Y-shaped tree and prop the longest branch you can find into the Y. This will be your den's frame. Lean other branches and sticks against this

long branch until you have a wall that shelters you from cold winds. You could put sticks on both sides of the branch to build two walls, but remember to leave a doorway so you can get in and out! Fill in the gaps between the branches with fallen leaves to make your den really cozy and windproof. Try experimenting to see what other types of dens you can build.

Variation

Build a fort in a similar way.

Mini Woodland *(ages 4 and up)*

Pretend you're a giant and design your own miniature woodland!

Supplies: Sticks, twigs, leaves, pinecones, rocks

On a patch of grass or dirt, build your woodland. Look around you for anything you can use to represent trees. Plant the "trees" where you want them. Add boulders, paths, benches, ponds or rivers, gates, fences, miniature sculptures, tiny dens, whatever you can think of.

Variations

- **Game:** Draw a map of your mini-woodland. Hide something tiny somewhere in it, mark it on the map, and see if a family member or friend can find the hidden treasure!
- PHOTOJOURNALIST: Take a picture of your woodland.
- NATURE JOURNAL: Give your woodland park a name and make up a story about it.
- **Sand Castle and Village:** Hanging out on the beach? You can make a castle or an entire city out of wet sand and a few cups, buckets, or whatever containers you

Psst . . . Kids! Make sure you always pay careful attention to what you're doing when you're whittling! That focus is part of what makes whittling so much fun, besides the obvious awesomeness of being able to use a knife.

pocketknife to shave and carve wood. Some folks say there's nothing more enjoyable than sitting around a campfire and whittling away at a twig while you talk to your buddies or family!

When whittling, carefully supervise your children. A pocketknife is a useful camping tool, but it is also sharp and takes time to learn how to control.

have. Use sticks to carve out windows and doors, and use sticks and rocks to add other features.

Whittling *(ages 8 and up)*

This fun and often relaxing outdoor activity goes way back and involves using a

Supplies:

- A sharpened pocketknife, such as a Swiss Army knife

- A twig or branch
- Adult supervision
- Duct-tape thumb pad

The Knife. Use a pocketknife with a sharp blade. It's not only easier to whittle if the blade is sharp, it's safer. Instead of cutting, dull blades have a tendency to glance off the wood and head right toward your hand. While the blade might not be sharp enough to cut wood, it's usually still sharp enough to cut through skin.

The Wood. When choosing sticks or branches, the general rule is to look for wood that is neither freshly cut (too much sap) nor very dry (breaks easily). When making more-advanced projects, look for branches with as few knots as possible and a small pith, the soft or spongy center of the branch. Softwoods are the easiest for whittling. These include basswood, pine, and balsa, but you should do fine with random twigs and branches. Wood with a straight grain is easier to whittle than wood that has the grain going in multiple directions.

Protect your hands. Even adults new to whittling often wear leather work gloves or leather thumb pads, but these are often too big for kids. A great solution that works just as well as leather is to make each child a duct-tape thumb pad. To avoid getting sticky stuff on your thumb, use the following technique.

How to Make a Duct-Tape Thumb Pad

- Wrap one layer of duct tape around your thumb with the sticky side facing out. Wrap it tight enough so it won't slip off, but not so tight that you lose circulation to your thumb.

- Then wrap a couple of layers of duct tape around your thumb with the sticky side facing in. Four or five layers should do the trick.

How to Whittle

1. **Take it slow.** No need to rush! Whittling is supposed to be relaxing and meditative. When you get in a hurry, that's when accidents happen. Make every cut slow and controlled.

2. **Cut with the grain of the wood when you can.** Sometimes it's easy to tell the direction of the grain on a piece of wood simply

by looking at it. But if it's not obvious, start making some small shallow cuts in your wood. *Cuts made with the grain will peel away smoothly; cuts made against the grain will give resistance and eventually split.*

3. **There are three basic whittling cuts.** If you're left-handed, just flip the directions.

   Straightaway Cutting. This cut is good for removing a lot of wood quickly. Hold the wood in your left hand and, using long, firm strokes, cut away from yourself with your right hand. It helps to lock your right wrist, not bending it, to control the cut. Don't cut too deep or you might split the wood. You'll use this cut

the most as a beginning whittler, and it's all you need to create roasting sticks for hot dogs and marshmallows.

Draw Cutting (also called Pull Stroke or Pare Cutting). This is the most frequently used cut in whittling. Place the wood in your left hand and the knife in your right. Cut toward yourself with short

Did You Know?

The most popular pocketknife in the world is the Swiss Army knife. Is it really from Switzerland, you may ask? Yes! During the late 1880s, the Swiss Army decided to purchase a new folding pocketknife for its soldiers. Soldiers needed one tool they could use for both opening canned food and assembling and disassembling the rifle they used, which required a screwdriver. The first Swiss Army knife had a blade, reamer (a tool for widening or finishing drilled holes), can opener, and screwdriver.

The term "Swiss Army knife" was created by US soldiers returning from World War II, who had trouble pronouncing its German name: *Schweizer Offiziersmesser* (Swiss officers knife).

Actually, in AD 200, the Romans invented their own Swiss Army–esque knife that included a spoon, blade, spike, fork, spatula, and pick. These most likely belonged to wealthy travelers.

strokes, a bit like peeling an orange or paring an apple, using your right thumb as a brace against the wood. This is where your duct-tape thumb pad is good to have on! Keep some wood between the blade and your thumb for safety. Longtime whittlers often keep their right thumbs braced on their left thumbs, not on top of the wood itself. That way, you don't run the risk of the blade coming up into your right thumb on its follow-through. The pull stroke gives you lots of control over your blade and is best for detailed cuts. Use this to shape a piece of wood into something else, like a human figure, animal, or wooden knife.

Thumb Pushing (Push Stroke). This is a great controlled stroke for small, precise cuts. Sometimes where you want to cut won't allow you to do the pull stroke. That's when it's time to bust out the push stroke. Hold the wood in your left hand and the knife firmly in your right hand, with the blade facing away from you. Place both your right and left thumbs on the back of the knife blade. Push the blade forward with your left thumb while your right thumb and fingers guide the blade through the wood.

Psst . . . Kids! What is the use of a walking stick? It can give you stability when you walk, especially on loose terrain. It can help you cross streams. For older folks, it relieves stress on the joints. A walking stick can give you a measure of security if you are a bit frightened by nature. It is, after all, a big, solid stick. It also can make you feel like a wizard with a staff, like a professional mountain climber, like a hobbit on an adventure, like Little John in the story of Robin Hood, or like a ninja. It can be a measuring stick (see page 153). You name it! You can also make it into an amazing journey stick (see page 175).

Find the Perfect Walking Stick
(ages 3 and up)

Going on a hike with the family? If kids aren't sure they want to go, here's a challenge that

Photo by Kevin Meynell

will help get them down the trail lickety-split: Try to find the perfect walking stick.

What is perfect for a walking stick? It has to be sturdy and pretty straight, although a curve for your grip would be great. It has to have some weight to it and be the right height—tall enough so you can grip it around the level of your belly button. (Think about the height of your arms when you walk and naturally swing them forward and back.) You might want to take the bark off where

Laugh Time!
Q: What bow can't be tied?
A: A rainbow!

Did You Know?

The Report on Rainbows

Isaac Newton discovered in 1666 that when he passed regular sunlight through a prism (a triangular piece of glass), the prism would split the light into a band of colors. The band of colors is called the spectrum, which appears in this order: red, orange, yellow, green, blue, indigo, and violet. Why? White light isn't just one color. It's a combination of all the visible colors. So when white light bends, all its components, the colors, also bend. Each color bends at a different angle because each color travels at a different speed. When it rains, the raindrops act like a prism. If sunlight passes through the raindrops at the proper angle, it is split into its spectrum, a rainbow. Sometimes you can find a rainbow in a puddle too. Try creating your own rainbow by holding a glass of water above a white sheet of paper or light-colored stone in direct sunlight. Watch as the light passes through the glass of water and forms a rainbow of colors on the paper. Move the paper or glass around a bit to get different reflections.

Got a mirror? Fill a shallow pan about halfway full with water. Place a mirror in the water at an angle so the sun can shine on the mirror underwater. Hold a white paper above the mirror, adjusting the angle until you see the rainbow appear.

you hold it. And you'll need to try it out on the trail. Find walking sticks for other family members.

Explore and Surprise with Camping Supplies

Invent, explore, experiment, and play using rocks, sticks, ropes, containers from your camping kitchen, and more combined.

Plant a Seed

Pretend you are a plant. How are you going to disperse your seeds?

Supplies:

- Pebbles, leaves, sticks
- Tape
- String and/or yarn
- Glue
- Optional: a variety of other materials like plastic bags, fabric, toilet paper tubes

You're a plant. The pebbles are your seeds. You have to plant them to survive. Figure out how you will disperse them given one of these situations:

1. If you plant it next to you, it will take your sunshine and nutrients, and you will die.
2. There are a lot of animals where you are that like to eat your seeds.
3. You produce very few seeds, so they need to have a good chance of surviving.
4. You need your seeds to travel some distance, because the conditions where you are no longer support plants like yourself.

5. You make lots of seeds and want to plant as many as possible.
6. Your seeds will only grow if they are in the ground.
7. What other situations can you come up with to determine how you will disperse your seeds?

Design your seed so that you can disperse it to survive your conditions. Experiment to see if your design works. Give yourself, as a plant, a name. Write about you and your seed in your NATURE JOURNAL. Be a PHOTOJOURNALIST and take a picture of your finished seed. Or pretend you are a botanist explorer and film a short documentary about the seed.

The Natural 10-Second Timer
  (ages 8 and up)

You can use gravity to tell time in this fun science experiment you can do in camp.

Supplies:

- Round rock
- Paper, tape
- Natural objects
- A log or slope
- Watch or stopwatch

The goal is to make a timer that measures exactly 10 seconds by using gravity and objects in nature or the camping kitchen. Create your timer by rolling a rock or ball down a fairly smooth surface. It could be a log with a concave side, a cutting board, cardboard, or even a hillside. Each time you do, release it the same way, and time it from release to some end

SEED DISPERSAL SYSTEMS

Plants have many methods of delivering seeds to the ground, sometimes sending them far away to start a new life. Most likely they use one of these seed dispersal systems:

- **Gravity.** Some plants simply let their seeds fall to the ground. But among these plants are ones that have burrowing seeds. Burrowing seeds are designed to twist and drill themselves into the soil. Wheat is one plant that does this.

- **Animals.** To disperse farther away, some seeds hitch a ride. These seeds are often covered with barbs or sticky mucous, perfect for attaching to unsuspecting passers-by. Some seeds, like those encased in tasty fruit, hitch a ride in the digestive systems of animals. Hard coatings allow them to pass through and emerge at the other end relatively unscathed. Or animals collect seeds, like nuts, dropping some on the ground.

- **Air.** Some plants have developed amazing designs to harness the wind. Their seeds spin and fly. Some float gently on a breeze, and others look like tiny parachutes. Some rely on the wind to bow their stalks and tip out seeds like a saltshaker. If the wind is right, seeds from certain plants can travel hundreds of miles. The problem is that most seeds don't fall in

point. It is best to use a stopwatch, but you can count as well (one 1,000, two 1,000 . . .). Adjust the angle of the surface until the object reaches the bottom in exactly 10 seconds several times in a row. Can you design a timer for a different amount of time?

Variation

Campground Hourglass. Create a longer timer, such as a 1-minute timer out of repurposed drink or food containers, paper, duct tape, and sand or dirt. You are basically creating your own hourglass timer. First build a contraption that funnels dirt or sand from one compartment into another. Then you will have to experiment to figure out how much sand or dirt to use to equal 1 minute. Test it several times for accuracy. Make your timer for 3 minutes or some other amount of time. You can use this for timed games in this book or as a cooking timer!

String and Cup Phone (ages 5 and up)

Who needs technology to call a friend when you've got a few camping supplies and sound waves!

Supplies:

- 2 paper or plastic cups
- string

suitable growing locations. To solve this problem, plants that use wind dispersal produce a lot of seeds. If you've made a wish on a dandelion puff, you have seen wind dispersal in action!

- **Water.** Plants near rivers, lakes, and oceans often use water to move their offspring. They have seeds that float, and the water carries them away—hopefully to a suitable growing location. This dispersal method explains how remote islands have vegetation similar to landmasses hundreds of miles away. Coconuts have developed seeds that can survive thousand-mile voyages at sea.

- **Mechanical.** Some plants have developed the ability to "launch" their seeds. These plants build up tension in their tissue, much like a catapult stores energy in a taut rope. At just the right moment, the tension is released and the seeds are flung. Some seeds shoot like tiny missiles.

- **Fire.** Some of the most remarkable seeds are those adapted to survive fires so intense the flames kill virtually everything else in their path. These seeds need to get burned in order to be released and grow. Intense heat explodes their seed cones and cracks their hard kernels, like popcorn, so that water can leak in and begin the growth process. Many trees where forest fires are common have fire cones.

Make a hole in the bottom of each cup. Take a long length of string, poke it through the bottom of each cup, and tie a knot on the inside. Now stretch it almost as far as it will go. Talk into your cup while the other person puts his or her ear to the other. The vibrations on the string will allow

the sound waves to travel from one cup to the other. You can even hear the other person whisper.

Rube Goldberg Machine *(ages 9 and up)*

A Rube Goldberg machine is a contraption that uses chain reactions to perform a very simple task in a very complicated fashion. They are super fun and challenging to build. Rube Goldberg was a cartoonist and inventor who liked to draw such devices in some of his cartoons. This is a great activity to do as a family or on your own.

Supplies:

- Duct tape
- String
- Anything from your camping gear
- Balls (optional)
- Sticks, rocks, and other natural objects

1. Make a machine of action and reaction out of natural objects and camping supplies (with permission). What it does, the final reaction, can be very simple. It could move a ball along a path or pick a fork off the table at the end. It's up to you.

2. Think of ways you can create natural force to move things and create chain reactions. Gravity, elasticity, water, and wind all work. Devices like a pulley or dominoes that knock into each other work well.

The idea is to put together a few of these devices so that they go off one right after the other, like a chain reaction. Once you put the first one in motion, the rest of the machine should go by itself.

Example:

Swinging a piece of wood on a string (attached to a tree branch) knocks down a water bottle on a table. The water from the water bottle hits a domino, which hits another, and eventually knocks them all down. The last domino hits a tennis ball that rolls downward at an angle on a track made of two sticks from the table to the bench. The tennis ball bumps into a table tennis ball on the bench, which falls over the edge into a cup of water below to make a big splash.

Hand Puppet Wildlife Show *(ages 3 and up)*

Welcome to the show! I'm your host! You can do this fun activity with or without a camera.

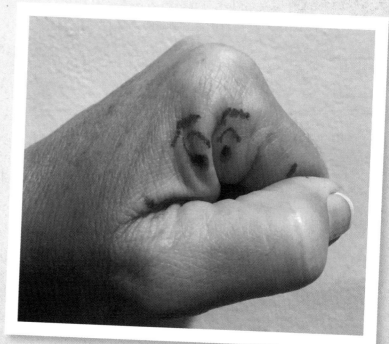

Supplies: Pen or some sort of marker; camera or smartphone video app (optional)

1. Make a fist with your thumb next to your index finger on the side. Move the thumb up and down to make a mouth. With a pen (or mud or cold charcoal from burnt wood), make eyes above the mouth.

2. Now National Geographic's Mr. Hand of the Wild and friends can go on great adventures to share with their television audience. Find cool stuff around camp, and narrate your discovery as though your hand is the host of a wildlife show.

3. If you have the capability to video segments, think about what you are going to say and film in short segments. Viewed at home, the video will add to the fun memories of the trip. It could be educational or just hilarious.

Variation
You can be the host instead of your hand!

Where's Waldo (or the Gnome)?

This PHOTOJOURNALIST activity requires a camera and can be ridiculously funny and silly.

Supplies: A figure, doll, toy, or trophy; a camera

Bring a doll, stuffed animal, or figurine from home. Or you could borrow one from a friend too. (Assume it will get a little dirty.) Take the figure with you on your camping adventures and take pictures of it in all kinds of different places, as if it were on vacation doing all the activities. Send these pictures to a friend, or make a scrapbook of them once you're back home.

Variations

- Have players close their eyes as you put the doll somewhere in the natural setting. Then players go seeking it.

- Try to camouflage the doll and take pictures from farther away. When you get home, print out the pictures to create your own *Where's Waldo?* book.

- Play Hotter–Colder by giving these clues when the seekers are nearing the item or getting farther away from it.

Tying Knots

Knots are important in outdoor recreation. You use them to tie up rain tarps, dock a boat, rig a fishing line, even put up a swing. They are essential to wilderness survival and mountain climbing. During downtime at the campsite is a great time to learn to tie some knots. You can motivate

the family to try some of these knots by offering to put up a hammock or a line to hang artwork from if they help you with the knots.

Though there are many varieties, here are three good, basic knots to begin with: square knot, clove hitch, and bowline knot. (If you get into knot tying—it can be fun and feel good to your hands—look up and try to do a taut-line hitch, a fisherman's knot, a double fisherman's knot, and an alpine butterfly loop.)

The Square Knot. Also known as the reef knot, it is easy to tie and very useful. You can tie bandages and packages and even use it to tie a rope belt to keep your pants up.

1. Hold a rope in each hand or the ends of one rope in each hand.

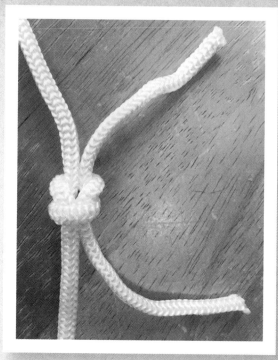

2. Tie an overhand knot as you would for tying your shoelaces, by putting the right end under and over the left rope end.

3. Then tie another overhand knot, this time putting the left end under and over the right rope.

4. Pull on both ends to tighten.

Clove Hitch. This knot is easy to tie and untie and will serve you well. You will need a post or tree to practice it on. It can slip or loosen if tension is released or if the post it is tied to moves a lot.

1. Wrap the free end of a rope around a post.

2. Cross the rope over itself and around the post again.

3. Slip the working end of the rope under the last wrap.

4. Pull tight.

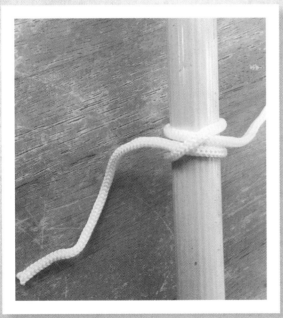

Bowline Knot. Every camper, sailor, or climber should know how to tie a bowline, which is sometimes called the king

of knots, because it is so useful. It is a very secure knot under tension but is easy to tie and untie. You can even learn how to do this knot one-handed if you're holding something with your other hand. Use it to secure a line around an object, such as a hammock or clothesline to a tree or to secure a boat to a mooring.

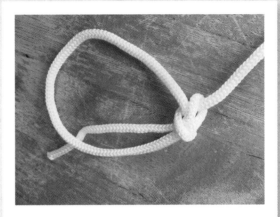

1. **The rabbit hole.** Lay the rope across your left hand with the free end hanging down. Form a small loop in the line in your hand.

2. **Out comes the rabbit.** Bring the free end up to and pass through the eye from the underside (the rabbit comes out of the hole).

3. **Runs around the tree.** Wrap the line around the standing line and back down through the loop (around the tree and back down the hole).

4. **And hops back into its hole.** Tighten the knot by pulling on the free end while holding the standing line.

Family Conversation Starters

- What is it like to be a kid? What is it like to be a parent? Do you think it's more fun to be a parent or a child?
- Do you know any stories about your grandparents when they were kids?
- What is your favorite silly face to make? Silly sound?
- If you could be an animal, what would you want to be? Why?
- In the famous "Marshmallow Study" by Stanford University, children were presented with one marshmallow or other treat, which they could either eat immediately or not eat for 15 minutes in order to get more. What do you think you would do?
- What would happen if the sun was always shining and it never rained?
- In general, do you think we as a society are more or less tolerant toward one another than we used to be? Why or why not?

CHAPTER 6
GAMES IN THE OUTDOORS

It's not just kids who learn through play and games. Though playing games is a natural and essential part of childhood development, both kids and adults need what games provide: laughter, downtime, camaraderie, and physical or mental exercise. Ask any artist or inventor. Playtime is when creativity and problem solving happens, the incubation of great ideas. And frolicking together builds goodwill, trust, and positive associations. We learn about one another through play, when we're most relaxed and ourselves. These games will help you explore your surroundings and interact with your family

> To me a lush carpet of pine needles or spongy grass is more welcome than the most luxurious Persian rug.
>
> —Helen Keller

Psst . . . Kids! Uncomfortable with competition? Play a game without keeping score or focus on strategy. Just have fun or try something new with your family. Remember: Winning doesn't equal being good, and losing doesn't equal being bad. It is okay to win against family members too. If you get mad about losing, take a deep breath and don't take it out on other people. Channel your anger into something positive, like winning the next game or hiking faster or helping your parents prepare the wood in the fire pit.

or with friends in healthy competitive or cooperative ways. Some will also provide a little introspective or downtime when you need a break from all the stimuli around you. Some will help you discover that you don't need much more than your imagination and a pencil and paper to have a whole lot of fun. Remember to model good sportsmanship!

Exploration Games
These games help you discover the world around you.

Scavenger Hunt! *(ages 2 and up; pair younger kids with older partners)*

Take this classic and make it new again in the campground or on the trail. There are many variations to try.

Supplies: Paper and pencil; bags to collect stuff in (optional)

Write down a list of items for players to hunt for. The player (or team) who finds the most items in the given amount of time (start with 15 minutes) wins. Consider including these items on your hunt list, or use this list to inspire your ideas: a rock shaped like a heart, a tree that smells like vanilla, a slug, lichen, a feather, a Y-shaped stick, a crawling insect, a flying insect, a purple flower, a piece of man-made garbage (pick it up and throw it away for a bonus!). You can also find pre-made nature scavenger hunts online to print out before leaving home.

Keep track of your scavenger hunt in your NATURE JOURNAL, or use it afterwards to describe other things you discovered and saw in the process or to press leaves and stuff you found. You can be a PHOTOJOURNALIST and take pictures of your scavenger hunt items, especially ones you cannot move. Take pictures of the hunters too for your post-camping slideshow.

Variations

- **Alphabet Scavenger Hunt.** Instead of a specific list of items, each camper finds something that starts with each letter of the alphabet and writes it in next to the appropriate letter. You can do this on

Photo by *Kevin Meynell*

the trail as a group and without paper by calling out the things you see that start with each letter. Take turns if one person is dominating.

- **Category Scavenger Hunt.** Instead of the alphabet, make a list of categories. **Examples:** animals, trees, flowers, man-made stuff, items found in nature, items of many colors (none can repeat).

- **Nature Only Scavenger Hunt.** A little more challenging, add the rule of no man-made objects, only things found in nature.

- **Theme Scavenger Hunt.** Even more challenging, all items must fit a theme. **Examples:** things that grow; things bigger than your head.

- **Creating a Hunt for the Parents.** Kids make up the list and send the parents off to find interesting and unique things.

- **Nighttime Scavenger Hunt.** Use your ears, eyes, and flashlights to find animals and things seen almost only at night. Include animals and night noises, such as owls, frogs, crickets, moths, spiders, or something with glowing eyes. You can also use objects in the night sky (the moon, a constellation) or man-made objects designed for the night, like reflective signs.

Memory Game Scavenger Hunt
(ages 4 and up)
Test your memory and go hunting for stuff! This is also fun during a hiking break.

Supplies: Stuff all around you, a jacket or bandana (something to cover items), paper and pencil

1. Take turns being the Game Host.

2. The Game Host secretly collects ten different items easily found in the environment. Some examples are a pinecone, acorn, rock, straight stick, forked stick, fallen tree leaf, a piece of kindling wood, even an item from the camping kitchen, like a spoon.

3. Put the items under something like a jacket, shirt, towel, or bandana.

4. The other campers gather around.

5. Uncover the items, let everyone look at them for 5 or 10 seconds, then cover them again.

6. Now send your campers out to find matching items in or around the campsite or trail. Set a 5- to 15-minute time limit. Campers can go individually or in pairs. Young campers should always go in pairs or with a parent-partner.

7. The person or team that returns with the most matching items wins.

The Bag of Mystery *(ages 2 and up)*
Players try to identify items in a bag just by touch.

Supplies: A bag (sleeping bag sack or pillowcase is fine) you can't see through; natural objects

1. Find an item or items around camp that have an interesting texture or might be hard to identify, or something that you think would be fun for your children to learn about. DO NOT INCLUDE ANYTHING THAT WILL BITE OR POKE INTO SMALL HANDS.

2. Player reaches in and tries to identify each object. This will enhance their sensory awareness.

3. Ask the player questions to encourage thoughtful exploration or engage the imagination: Can animals use the object as food? Where do you find the object? What color do you think it is? Does it grow? What is its texture like? Does it feel like something else? What could you do with it?

I Spy *(ages 3 and up)*

This classic game is great on the trail or in camp, where you have an entirely different world than at home.

1. One person spots an object and announces it with a one-word clue. Something like: "I spy something blue."

2. The other campers get to ask up to three questions that can be answered with a yes or a no and try to guess what the item is.

3. If no one guesses it, the spotter gives them another clue, like: "I spy something blue way up high."

4. Campers get three more yes-or-no questions.

5. If no one gets it right again, then a third clue can be given. If the item still isn't guessed, the spotter points out what was "spied" and takes another turn.

6. A camper who guesses an item gets to "spy" the next object.

Variations

- Limit the objects to a category like plants or wildlife or something from home.

- Instead of giving clues describing the object "spied," the clues can be objects near or related to the object. **Example: If** the object is a tree stump, a clue might be "I spy a fallen tree." If the object is a hiking trail sign, a clue might be "I see a fork in the trail."

Only Nature Needed

These games require only found objects from nature and your enthusiasm!

Campground Bocce Ball *(ages 2 and up)*

This traditional Italian bowling game can be adapted to play on the beach or in a clear space in the campground and is a lot of fun to play with the family or even as a one-person challenge!

Supplies:

- 8 rocks

- Another larger or smaller rock to serve as the "jack"

- Measuring tape (optional)

- A cleared space in packed dirt or moist sand about 20 × 5 feet or longer if possible (but you can make do with less space)

Bocce is played with eight large balls and one smaller target or object ball called the "jack" (in this case the odd-size rock will serve as the jack). Create 2 sets of 4 rocks by using rocks of different colors or marking 4 of them with a strip of duct tape. Players take turns tossing the jack-rock before each round. The object is to have one of your rocks closest to the jack. Two or 4 players take turns tossing their rocks

Supplies:

- Knee-high or taller sturdy sticks
- Small ball-like rocks, pinecones, wadded-up paper, or balls
- Various natural obstacles
- Flat-sided rocks and duct tape (optional)

underhand toward the jack. When all eight rocks have been played, check the distance to the jack, collect the rocks, and start the next round. The winner, closest to the jack, receives 1 point. First player to reach 10 points wins the game.

Variation

- Use eight tennis balls and one golf ball for the jack and roll them. Like in real bocce, you can knock your opponent's ball away as well as roll closest to the jack.

Nature Minigolf *(ages 3 and up)*
Create your own natural miniature golf course. Setting up this game is half the fun! You can play it with the whole family.

Make your golf clubs. Find a rather fat stick. If it is too wet or rotted, it might break too easily. Use as is, or whittle one side of your stick at the bottom to create a flat surface—the face of your club, where you'll hit the ball (see "Whittling" page 96). Or get out the old duct tape and wrap a rock with a flat surface on the outside to the bottom of your stick. (Make sure to remove duct tape when you pack up camp.) You could also make yourself a duct-tape grip.

Make your balls. Find round rocks or small pinecones. Probably the easiest to control would be a ball made from wadded and wound duct tape or a combination of paper and duct tape. You could use tennis balls or golf balls from home too.

Create your course. Scout the area to create your holes and add some fun challenges.

You might have to zig and zag around brush and plants or hit the ball around a tree or even along a decomposing log. You will probably have to experiment with each hole, changing them up for maximum fun and challenge. If you are clearing an area for your hole, leave the live plants as obstacles and only clear the debris and dead stuff.

Take your time. You can take several hours or several days to set up your course and improve upon it and then play it as many times as you wish while camping. If creating the course as a family, you could have each person make up a hole.

Mark the tee box. Put rocks on either side of the space where each hole starts. Number your holes on the rocks with chalk or charcoal, or write on a strip of tape. (Remove and throw away later.)

Dig the holes. Use a small shovel, stick, or kitchen utensil/cup (with permission) to dig a hole deep enough for the ball to fall into, at least 2 or 3 inches deep. You can also incorporate used cans and cups and boxes from your camping kitchen. If you have paper, you can make triangle flags, tape them to sticks, and poke them into or near your holes.

Rock Toss-a-Cross *(ages 5 and up)*

Make three in a row by tossing rocks into squares!

Supplies: Rocks and sticks

1. Clear a square of ground, about 2 × 2 feet or bigger. Carving the ground with a stick, divide the square into nine smaller squares. If the ground is too tough to carve, you can place sticks or shape piles of pine needles to create the squares. Collect six rocks about the same size. If possible, find three of one color and three of another so that you can tell them apart. If you can't find different-looking rocks, with a pen, paint, or mud, mark three rocks with an O and three rocks with an X.

2. Two players take turns tossing their rocks underhand into the squares. The player that gets three in a row (vertically, horizontally, or diagonally) wins the round. Play multiple rounds up to 10 points. You can also make up your own tossing goals, like four corners or the shape of a C. (You'll need more rocks for these!)

Chinese Jacks or Gonggi Noli
(ages 5 and up)

This is a jacks game popular in Korea and China. *Gonggi* means "air." *Noli* means "play" or "game." With no jacks or balls, you can still play a great game of jacks. All you need are five pebbles and a quick hand!

Supplies: 5 pebbles or pennies

Game Play:

1. Drop the five pebbles on the ground or other flat surface.

2. Pick up one pebble and toss it into the air. Quickly pick up another pebble and catch the one you tossed in the air.

3. Now with two pebbles in your hand, throw one of the pebbles in the air and pick up a third.

4. This goes on until you have all the pebbles in hand.

5. In the second round, pick up two pebbles every time you throw one into the air.

6. In the third round, pick up three; four in the fourth round. The fifth time, pick them all up.

7. In the final round (optional), toss the stones into the air and try to catch them on the back of your hand. Then throw them off the back of your hand and turn your hand over to try to catch them all in your palm.

8. The number of pebbles you catch is your score.

Rules:

- If you touch any pebbles other than the one you are picking up, it's the next person's turn.

- If you drop any pebble while catching, it's the next person's turn.

- If you fail to catch all the pebbles during the last round, it's the next person's turn.

Nature Hopscotch *(ages 2 and up)*

You don't need pavement for this classic blacktop game.

Supplies: A stick and rocks

Most people know the basic game of hop-scotch. You can create your own hopscotch course by tracing the squares in dirt and tossing a rock on the square to skip. Played all over the world, here are some hopscotch games you might not know.

Variations

- **Kick Hopscotch.** On your way back from home base, kick the stone sequentially back through the course on the return trip.

It has to land in the next square without touching a line or rolling out.

- **Spiral Hopscotch.** Play a French variant of hopscotch called escargot (snail) or *marelle ronde* (round hopscotch). It is played on a spiral course. Players must hop on one foot to the center of the spiral and back out again. If the player reaches the center without stepping on a line or losing balance, the player marks one square with his or her initials. From then on, that player may place two feet in his or her initialized or "owned" square while all other players must hop over it. The game ends when all squares are marked or no one can reach the center; the winner is the player who "owns" the most squares.

- **Heaven and Hell Hopscotch.** Play it like they do in Germany, Austria, and Switzerland, where they most commonly call hopscotch *Himmel und Hölle* (Heaven and Hell). The first square is called *Erde* (Earth). The second to last square is the *Hölle* (Hell), and the last one is *Himmel* (Heaven). Besides your square with the rock, no one can step on the square of hell!

- **Quarter-Square Hopscotch.** Create a course like those made in 1900. Along with single and double squares, in one large square, draw an X to divide it into four corners. Number these with the rest, dropping your stone and hopping on each in order.

- **Australian Hopscotch.** In Australia, hopscotch is played in rounds. The first round is played by hopping per the standard rules. The next round is called "jumps," and the player jumps into each square with two feet. The last round is called "sizzles," and you jump into each square with your legs crossed. The first player to complete all three stages wins. Younger players can use "helps," lines extended at the sides between squares 2 and 3 so little ones can get closer to throwing the stone into the required square.

Did You Know?

Jumpin' Fun Facts about Hopscotch!

Hopscotch is a really old game! Children in ancient Rome (around AD 700) played a form of hopscotch. The first references to the game in the English-speaking world date back to the late 1600s, when it was called "scotch-hop" or "scotch-hoppers." Hopscotch is known by many names. In Poland it is called *Klasy* (meaning class). In Italy children call it *Campana* (bell) or *Mondo* (world). In Mexico it is known as *Bebeleche* (mamaleche), meaning "drink milk" or *Avioncito*, meaning "little plane."

The current Guinness World Records holder for the fastest hopscotch game is actually an adult named Ashrita Furman, at 1 minute and 8 seconds. He has set over 550 Guinness World Records. Around 200 remain unbroken. If you can jump, you're never too old for hopscotch!

- **Crazy Course Hopscotch.** Instead of squares in a line, take your hopscotch course in any direction you want. It could form a V or even circle around a tree!

- **Hopscotch Truth or Dare.** In one round, players are required to answer a question or do or say something in each square before moving on. Examples are quack like a duck; turn in a circle on one foot (if you touch a line, you lose your turn); tell your favorite animal and why; tell where was your favorite place to travel and why; standing where you are, point at something blue.

Mancala (ages 5 and up)

Make and play this fun game (with hundreds of variations) with pebbles and holes in the ground, just like it was played in ancient times and is still played in parts of the world, like Africa. In Mancala (man-KAH-luh) you move your pebbles from hole to hole, trying to gather the most to be the winner of the game.

Supplies:

- 36 to 72 pebbles (or shells, beans, seeds, marbles, beads, or pennies)

- A stick or rock or small shovel to dig holes in the ground

- Instead of the ground (optional), use a repurposed egg carton and 2 cups, or 12 cups and 2 plates

Make your game board on the ground by digging twelve shallow bowls in the dirt or sand in two rows of six or drawing twelve circles with a stick. The bowls or circles should be big enough to hold twelve or fifteen of the pebbles comfortably in each bowl or circle. Dig a

bigger bowl at each end. These bigger bowls are called mancalas (or *kalahas*). This is where you will store all your captured pebbles.

For your game pieces, collect thirty-six to seventy-two pebbles, depending on the variation of the game you choose to play. This first variation requires forty-eight.

Sit on the ground so that you are facing six bowls. Your opponent sits opposite you. The six bowls nearest to you are yours. You can move any of the pebbles from your side, but you may not move your opponent's. The mancala on your right is yours as well.

Flip a coin or *ro sham bo* to see who goes first. Or use the traditional method in Africa to decide who goes first: One player holds a pebble in her fist. If the opponent correctly guesses which fist holds the pebble, the opponent starts.

Place four pebbles in each small bowl. The larger mancala bowl remains empty.

Game Play

1. The object of the game is to be the player with the most pebbles in the mancala.

2. At the start of each turn, a player picks up the pebbles in any of her small bowls. She then places one pebble in each small bowl, moving to the right, or counterclockwise.

3. The player should place a pebble in her own mancala but not in the opposing player's mancala as she goes around.

4. If the player drops her last pebble in a bowl with other pebbles in it, anywhere on the board, she picks them all up and proceeds to put one pebble in each bowl (except her opponent's mancala), moving to the right.

5. If she drops the last pebble in her mancala, she can pick up pebbles from any of the bowls on her side and keep going. If she drops the last pebble in a bowl that is empty, her turn is over.

6. Player #2 picks up pebble from his side and takes his turn the same way.

7. If a player has no more pebbles in his bowls at the start of a turn, the turn goes to the other player.

8. Play until all bowls—except the mancalas—are empty of pebbles.

Variations

- Start the game with three or five pebbles in each small bowl.

- Change the number of small bowls to four or five.

- Players may choose to drop stones in either direction. If the last pebble is placed in a bowl with other pebbles, the player picks up all of the pebbles and drops them in the opposite direction. This continues back and forth until the last pebble is dropped into an empty bowl.

- Play the game with four people, two on each side, either individually or in teams, following all other rules for dropping pebbles.

- Research and choose elements from any Mancala game, or make up your own to create your own specialized game. Just make sure all players agree with the rules.

Pick Up Sticks *(ages 6 and up)*
This is another classic made more fun by collecting sticks off the ground first.

Supplies: Sticks

Dump your sticks on the ground or table. Try to pick up a stick without disturbing any others. If you succeed, your turn continues. If you move another stick while picking up yours, the turn goes to the next player. Continue until all the sticks are picked up. The winner is the one with the most sticks.

Did You Know?

Mad Mancala Facts!
Mancala dates back at least 4,000 years! It is one of the oldest strategy board games in the world. The word *mancala* comes from the Arabic word *naqala*, meaning literally "to move." Mancala in its hundreds of variations is still played almost everywhere in the world and is especially popular in Africa, the West Indies, India, and Arabia. A version called *Giuthi* (guy-OO-thee) is most popular in Kenya, and *Oware* (Oh-WAH-ree) Mancala is the national game of Ghana.

Laugh Time!
Q: What do you call a boomerang that doesn't come back?
A: A stick.

Twig-Tac-Toe *(ages 5 and up)*

Make this classic game out of sticks and rocks, and try some variations of the game.

Supplies:

- Sticks
- 4 to 8 pebbles
- 8 small sticks or twigs; string (optional)

On the ground or table, lay out sticks to create a tic-tac-toe board, a grid of nine squares. The pebbles are your Os. Find rocks of a different color or mark them with an X for the Xs. Or use string to tie together smaller sticks to create your Xs. Three in a row wins!

Variations

- **Toe-Tac-Tic.** In this backward twist on the classic, try NOT to get three in a row. The first person to get three in a row loses

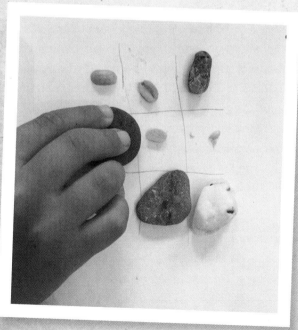

the game. It is a draw if neither player ends up with three in a row.

- **Tic-Tac-Toe in a sixteen-square grid.** Try to get either three or four across in a larger grid. This is similar to the classic game Connect Four.
- You can do these games on paper too.

Doggy, Doggy, Where's Your Bone? *(ages 2 and up)*

Be a doggy detective and get your bone back in this group guessing game.

Supplies: Small stick or rock

1. One person plays the part of the dog.
2. He sits in a chair with his back to the rest of the players. A small stick or rock is put under the chair. That is the bone.
3. While the dog has turned around with his eyes closed, another player sneaks up, steals the bone, hides it somewhere on her person, and sits down again.
4. Then everyone sings: "Doggy, Doggy, where's your bone? Somebody's stole it from your home. Guess who it might be!"
5. The dog has three chances to guess who took it.
6. If the dog guesses right, he gets to do it again. If he guesses wrong, the person who had the bone gets a turn as the dog.

Pinecone Hockey and Other Sports *(ages 6 and up)*

You don't need ice or a grass field to play Pinecone Hockey.

- Sturdy sticks for each player
- Pinecone or duct-tape "puck"

Find a fairly clear area of dirt, sand, or grass. You can play around obstacles if you have to. Create your goals with stumps, trees, and rocks already there, or mark them on the ground with sticks or rocks. Decide on the boundaries of your play field.

Find yourself a good sturdy stick to be your hockey stick. Find a pinecone, or make a ball out of duct tape (a tennis ball makes for a faster game). Divide into two teams. The game works best if you can have at least three people on each team.

Start with a face-off at the centerline. Play it like hockey, using your stick to hit your pinecone so it rolls in the direction you want it to go on the ground. *An important safety rule: Never swing your hockey stick above your knees.* One of the challenges is that the pinecone may not go exactly where you want it to go because of its shape and unevenness. Decide on a length of time for your game or that the first team to reach a certain score wins.

Variations

- **Pinecone Soccer.** Use a pinecone as your ball, and kick it to move it forward.

Chances are, at some point the pinecone will break apart. This is just part of the game. Replace it with another one at any time.

- **Pinecone Hacky Sack.** Don't have a Hacky Sack or a ball? You can still play hacky with a pinecone. Its weird bounce adds a challenge. Bounce it off your knees, feet, chest, or shoulders to another player. Try to keep it in the air. This game is not recommended if you're in your swimsuit. Too prickly! (You can substitute a duct-tape ball. Put a small rock in the center for a little weight.)

Stick Bowling *(ages 4 and up)*
Go for a strike and knock down all your sticks!

Supplies: Sticks and a round rock

You'll need a clear dirt path to be your alley. Gather ten sticks about the same length. At the end of your alley, poke or pound the sticks (with a rock) into the ground just so far that they stand up. They should be in a pyramid shape, with a single pin in the first row. Find as round a rock as possible. At the other end of your alley, roll that rock to try to knock down as many sticks as possible. Keep score just like indoor bowling, adding up the number of pins you knock down, with each player getting two turns to knock down the pins before setting them back up for the next player.

Variation
Use fewer sticks and different configurations of sticks. Try rolling a pinecone or a duct-tape ball.

Ulu Maika *(ages 2 and up)*

This is a fun traditional Hawaiian game that's a little like bowling. It used to be played with slices of a green breadfruit called *ulu* and wooden stakes.

Supplies:

- 2 sticks or other markers
- A disc-shaped rock (about 3 inches in diameter and 1 inch thick), pinecone, or duct-tape ball

Mark off a course of flat ground about 15 feet in length. For little children, the distance can be shorter. Pound two sticks in the ground about 6 inches apart. You can also use two 2-liter soda bottles full of water. Find your game stones. Roll the stones over the course aiming for the two sticks. The winner will be the one that is able to roll the stones in between the sticks without touching them.

Nim *(ages 8 and up)*

Don't be the last person to pick up a pebble in this game of mathematical strategy. Different versions of Nim have been played since ancient times. The game is thought to have originated in China, but the game's name, Nim, is a German word for "take."

Supplies: Pebbles, seeds, pennies, or sticks for game pieces

Set up your game pieces in three different rows or piles (called heaps in Nim). You can put any number of pieces into each of the three heaps. Players take turns picking up pieces. You can take as many as you'd like during your turn, but only from one heap. In other words, if you pick up 3 pieces, you cannot pick up 1 from one heap and 2 from another. You can only take 3 from the same heap. The person who is left with the last piece loses the game.

Variation

Play the opposite objective: be the last person to pick up a piece and win the game.

> **Psst . . . Kids!** Add a tasty element of fun to any game played with small markers on a tabletop. Instead of pebbles, use almonds, peanuts, blueberries, pretzels, chocolate pieces, or some other small snack food as markers. When the game is over, eat your winnings!

By Air, Land, or Sea *(ages 5 and up)*

This game combines reaction, memory, and movement for a lot of fun! It's especially fun with three or more players.

1. One person starts as the Caller.
2. Use a stick to make a line on the ground, or lay a stick down to be the line.
3. The Caller calls out the commands: **Land, Sea,** or **Air.**

Rules:

- **Land:** Everyone jumps behind the line.
- **Sea:** Everyone jumps over the line.
- **Air:** Everyone jumps up in place.
- If Land or Sea is called twice in a row, you don't move the second time.
- If Air is called twice in a row, jump up both times.

- If you jump on the line or make a mistake, you're out.
- The last person still jumping is the winner.

Pass the Stick *(ages 3 and up)*

While everybody chants a rhyme in this group game, don't be the one with the stick this time!

- Find a stick a foot long or shorter without any pointy bits.
- Everyone needs to learn this rhyme:

  Pass the Stick is the name
  Now it's time to play the game
  Better go fast as you can
  So it touches everyone's hand
  S-T-I-C-K spells stick!

1. Players sit in a circle or around a table.
2. Players pass the stick around the circle while saying the rhyme.
3. The person left holding the stick at the end of the rhyme is out.
4. Keep going until there is only one person left. That person is the winner!

Limbo *(ages 3 and up)*

Make sure to stretch before you Limbo. Now, how low can you go?!

Supplies:

- A long stick
- Music, recorded or live (optional)

Two players hold the limbo stick while the other players take turns going under it. Start it fairly high. To be a limbo, you have to lean backwards, not forwards. After each player goes under once, the bar is lowered about an

---

Did You Know?

The Limbo Like It Is

Limbo is a traditional popular dance contest that originated on the island of Trinidad. It got its name in the 1950s, but the limbo dates back to the 1800s in Trinidad. Traditionally the limbo dance began at the lowest possible bar height and the bar was gradually raised, signifying an emergence from death into life. In its adaptation to the world of entertainment, dance troupes began reversing the traditional order. R&B singer-songwriter Chubby Checker, who popularized the Twist, also popularized the limbo dance and the phrase "How low can you go?" The world record for the lowest limbo dance is only 8.5 inches above the ground!

---

inch. Players keep limboing under the limbo stick as it gets lower and lower. If you touch the stick with any part of your body, you're out. The last person left is the winner.

This is even more fun to music, so turn on your iPod or sing and play a tune for the limbo dancers.

Variation

You can play solo limbo by laying a stick over rocks or stumps that support it on either end.

Jump the Creek *(ages 3 and up)*

The creek keeps getting wider. Can you jump to the other side?

Supplies: 2 long sticks

To play, you have to set up the creek. Place the sticks on the ground about a foot apart. Players take turns trying to jump over the creek. If they land on or in the middle of the creek, they're out. When everyone has jumped once, move the sticks about another foot apart. The person who is able to jump the farthest without falling into the creek is the winner.

Read My Mind *(ages 8 and up)*

Got a lively and creative group of campers? See if they can guess the Secret Word!

Supplies: 5 rocks, leaves, or other natural "counters" for each player

Start everyone off with five counters. One person thinks of a noun—any noun (person, place, thing, or concept). This is the Secret Word. Everyone else makes a random guess as to what the noun may be. When all have guessed, the first player announces her word, and the others must all explain how the words they guessed relate to the Secret Word. For instance, if the Secret Word was *chair* and the guess was *horse*, the guesser could say that both have four legs and a person sitting on them. Each explanation is given a thumbs-up or thumbs-down by the other players. A majority of thumbs-downs means the guesser loses one counter. If everyone gets a thumbs-down on a given round, the player who thought of the Secret Word forfeits a counter. The person with the most counters left at the end of the game wins.

Family Conversation Starters

- Tell me your favorite story about our family. Why do you like this story in particular?
- If you met a group of aliens who were very different from you, how would you treat them?
- Imagine you are in the woods by yourself for a whole day. Where would you sleep? What would you eat?
- Would you rather be good-looking, smart, or athletic?
- Do you believe in love at first sight?
- What is the strangest word you've ever heard? What does it mean?

Game Time with Camping Supplies

Add camping supplies or a ball to play these games.

Nature Bingo *(ages 5 and up)*

This fun bingo game uses names of things found in nature instead of numbers. It's fun to set up and play.

Supplies:

- Paper, pens or pencils
- Scissors (optional)
- Pebbles or pennies
- Bowl
- Gallon-size ziplock bag (for storage)

Designate a Caller. Gather a lot of pebbles (twenty to twenty-five per player), and hand out a sheet of paper to all players. (Consider having a couple players make extra bingo cards.) Create your bingo cards by making a grid on a paper that is five rows of squares and five columns of squares (twenty-five squares). Leave room at the top! Make your grid large enough so you have room to write in each square. In the center square, write "FREE." (There are templates for blank bingo cards online that you can bring with you from home.)

Players help come up with five categories of things in nature or to do with camping. **Examples:** birds, mammals, trees, insects, fish, stuff in the tent, names of people in your family. (You can also use non-nature categories. You can even use word groups, such as emotions or exclamations.) Everyone writes the same five categories above each column of squares. The Caller writes them on a piece of paper to keep track.

Now players name items that fit in the first category, a minimum of eight, and write five of them randomly in the boxes in that column. The Caller writes them all down so she will be able to call out, for example, Bird—eagle.

Repeat this for all the columns, leaving your FREE space in the center.

Now you are ready to play! The Caller can cut out all the items and put them into a bowl or just randomly select from his master list. If the Caller has the item, he covers its space with a rock. The first player to cover five squares in a row, across, down, or diagonally wins the round.

Variations

- **Four Corners.** The first player to cover the four corners wins.
- **The Big C.** The first player to make the letter C on her card, by covering all the squares in the top row, bottom row, and left column, wins.
- **Black Out.** The first player to cover the entire card wins.
- **The Big O.** The first player to make the letter O on his card, by covering all the squares in the top row, bottom row, left and right columns, wins.
- **Picture Nature Bingo.** Using pictures, you can play bingo with really young campers. There are free versions online that you can print out, or make bingo cards of your own at home before you leave. Make sure you print out one extra card and cut it up for the caller.
- Make up a game of your own!

Hop the Rock *(ages 5 and up)*

You don't need to bring a game board, and you can play this checkers-like game with an opponent or alone.

Supplies:

- Paper
- Pencil or pen
- 14 pebbles

Draw a big triangle on a piece of paper. Then draw fifteen circles in five rows inside the triangle. The top row should have one circle; second row, two circles; third row, three;

fourth row, four; and the bottom should have five.

Gather your game pieces and take turns putting one pebble in each circle, leaving one circle without a pebble. You choose which one.

To play, find a pebble that can hop over another one into the empty space. Then you can take away the pebble that you've hopped over. You can hop diagonally, horizontally, or vertically. Hop more than once if you can! Whoever has the most pebbles at the end wins.

As a solo game, when you can't move anymore, count the number of pebbles left. The goal is to have the least number of pebbles remaining. Keep playing until you beat your record.

Draw & Tell *(ages 6 and up)*

One player has to get the other players to guess a phrase by drawing a picture.

The team that goes first chooses an artist. The other team secretly writes down a common phrase and shows it to that artist. The artist then has to get the other members of her own team to guess the phrase by drawing a picture. She is not allowed to give clues by talking or drawing letters or symbols.

Towel Ball Toss *(ages 6 and up)*

Whether on the beach or in camp, this is a fun one!

Supplies:

- Duct-tape ball, tennis ball, beach ball, or other soft ball

- 2 towels (bath or beach size for 4 players, hand towels for 2 players)

Two people hold each beach towel, one person at each end (or each person holds a hand towel, a hand on each end or 4 people hold the corners). Put some distance between the two teams. One team puts the ball in their towel. Using the towel, that team works together to throw the ball to the other team, which tries to catch the ball in their towel. Play catch back and forth.

If a team doesn't catch the ball, the other team gets a point, like in volleyball. The first team to get 3 points wins. If doing this at camp, be careful not to drop the towel on the ground. A clean towel is a camper's friend!

Forest Sweep *(ages 2 and up)*

We've placed this activity in the Games chapter to really help make cleaning up camp fun. Everyone gets a garbage bag or container. Players have 5 or 10 minutes (or any length of time) to collect as many pieces of garbage as they can find in a designated area. Everyone is a winner! You decide how to score and reward: an M&M for every piece of garbage or a piece of gum for every ten pieces. Or Dad has to dance a jig!

Trash Lacrosse *(ages 6 and up)*

Get clever repurposing camp trash into ball scoops to play this game of catch!

Supplies:

- Empty 2-liter plastic soda bottles, milk cartons, or jugs (any size), or even mac and cheese, cereal, or cracker boxes—any kind of container no longer needed

- Pinecone or duct-tape ball or tennis ball (rocks for older kids only)
- Duct tape
- Scissors or pocketknife (with adult supervision)
- Sticks (optional)

Find your containers to repurpose. Find a pinecone, rock, or ball that you will be able to catch and throw with the containers. To make the scoops, carefully cut the bottoms off the milk jugs, or cut off the tops of boxes and cut one side shorter in a crescent shape.

If the container doesn't have a handle, make one with duct tape. Cut one strip; cut a smaller strip and lay it on the larger one in the center, sticky side to sticky side. Use the sticky sides remaining to stick the tape strip to your container where you want your handle so that it curves up from the container, leaving room for your hand. Add more duct tape as needed to secure the handle and make it more comfortable. To make your containers into lacrosse sticks, attach a sturdy stick. (If creating lacrosse sticks, don't use a rock. They really fling your ball.)

Using your scoops and your ball of choice, play catch with your partner. Each time you catch the ball, take one step backward. See how far apart you and your partner can go and still catch the ball. Keep your eye on the ball!

Marshmallow Fling *(ages 3 and up)*

Unless you have a lot of campers, it's a rare thing to actually finish an entire bag of marshmallows on a camping trip. Set those extra marshmallows sailing, and have a partner catch them to win!

Supplies:

- Marshmallows
- Plastic spoons (or sticks)
- Small bags, like brown paper lunch bags; quart or gallon plastic bags; small pots and pans; or other containers around that size

If you have more than three players, split into teams of two. Each team has a marshmallow flinger (spoon) and a marshmallow catcher (bag).

Mark the flinging line on one end of your playing area. About 10 feet away, outline two 2-foot squares on the dirt, grass, or pavement. These are the boxes that the marshmallow catchers stand in.

The marshmallow flinger has to use the plastic spoon to fling marshmallows to his teammate, the catcher. The catcher holds the lunch bag and tries to catch her partner's marshmallows, but she can't leave her catcher's box. The first team to catch five or ten (the number is up to you) marshmallows in their bag wins. Make sure you clean up all the marshmallows—and don't eat them after they've been on the ground!

Variations

- Allow younger players to toss their marshmallows underhand.
- Make a different kind of flinger. You could try making a "flingshot" out of a Y-shaped stick and rubber bands, for instance.

Mini–Campground Olympics

(ages 6 and up)

The real Olympic Games include many different sporting events where the best athletes in the world compete. You can create your own miniature Campground Olympics and try to beat your best record or compete with other campers. Let the games begin!

Create a variety of events. Here are a few to try; be sure to make up some of your own events too.

Supplies:

- Woodland debris
- Duct tape
- Bucket, bowl, pot, or plastic container of water
- Spoon
- Paper and pencil
- String
- Rubber bands
- Various other camping supplies
- A watch, stopwatch, or timer

For each competitor, keep track of your events and times on a sheet of paper. Choose a country you will represent. Create "medals" for the winners. Make them out of paper or use nature prizes, or make rock or acorn necklaces (see page 183).

Opening Ceremonies. Make the flag of your country and sing its anthem. If you don't know the flag or anthem, make them up. The anthem can even be a rap or chant. All competitors get a chance to display their flag, sing their anthem, and wave to the spectators.

Long Jump. Your competitor is rock solid and in fine form. It is a rock. Create a lever (a seesaw) out of a flat piece of wood and another rock, or use a camp spoon balanced over a rock or stick to launch your rock. Measure the distance it jumps.

Javelin. Throw small sticks, toothpicks, or cotton swabs. Make a line with a stick, or tape a strip of duct tape about 3 feet away. Try to throw three "javelins" as close to the tape as you can without going past it. The player who throws a javelin closest to the line wins the event.

Swimming. Fill the longest container you have with water to be your Olympic pool. Or you can use a lake or other body of still water, determining your start and finish line. If you have a cork or two, use those; otherwise make a duct-tape base or use some other small object that floats, like a piece of wood. Draw a small face of your Olympic swimmer, cut it out, and tape it on top. This will be your sail, so you might want to keep it in a rectangular or square shape. If you need to, you can use a small stick to help it stand upright. On "Go!" blow your swimmer across the water. The first to make it to the other side wins.

400-Centimeter Dash. Also known as the 4-yard dash. Mark two lines with a stick or tape about 4 yards (12 feet) apart. Use duct tape to make little running shoes that fit on the ends of your fingers. (You can wrap thinner strips of tape around a pebble and the tip of your finger.) Make running shorts for your fingers too out of duct tape or paper taped onto your fingers. Now your Olympic runner is dressed and ready. On "GO!" get those fingers (or legs) moving and race your competitor to the finish line. Make sure you keep your fingertips on the ground or table at all times or you will be disqualified. First one to the finish line or the best time wins.

Archery. Make your targets out of paper by drawing concentric circles. Hang or prop them up. Try to hit the target with rubber bands. The archer who hits the target five times is the winner.

High Dive. Fill two camping mugs or cups with water. Collect twenty small rocks or pennies. Put the cups on the ground a couple feet away from where you will stand. Stand on the picnic table bench (or cooler or hard chair) and toss your rocks into the cup of water below. The country to get the most pebbles into the cup wins the event.

Soccer. Set up your soccer field on a table or on top of your cooler. Make your soccer ball about the size of your fingernail; make it out of paper or duct tape or use a small, round rock. Use tape or sticks to mark your goalposts. Sit across from one another and flick the ball with your fingers. Play for 5 minutes. The team with the most goals wins.

Award Ceremonies. Present medals to the winners, repeating your anthem and cheering.

Nature Chopstick Pick-Up *(ages 3 and up)*

Use your chopstick savvy to pick up all the rocks and win the game! Don't know how to use chopsticks? You will after this game! (Don't worry! You can also use "cheater" chopsticks!)

Supplies:

- Sticks (or chopsticks)
- Small rocks and/or a variety of small natural objects
- A bowl or plate for each player (or 2)

- Rubber band (or duct tape) and piece of paper for cheater chopsticks (optional)

If you don't have chopsticks, find a pair of sticks you can you use as chopsticks, and whittle off the bark. Collect a whole bunch of small rocks. You can also use acorns, small pinecones, leaves, small sticks, and other natural objects. Divide them up among the players. You might start with ten each. The number is up to you. Players put their objects on a plate or in a pile on the table or ground in front of them.

All players need an empty bowl or plate to deposit their objects on after picking them up. Players have 30 seconds to see how many objects they can pick up with their chopsticks and transfer to their empty bowl. If playing with single player or younger players, race against the clock instead of one another.

How to hold chopsticks. Put one of the chopsticks in your hand and hold it just like you hold a pencil. Now put the other chopstick between your thumb and index finger. Move your thumb and index finger back and forth so the pointy ends of the chopsticks touch.

How to make cheater chopsticks:

1. Wrap the top of the sticks or chopsticks tightly with a rubber band to secure them together. If you don't have a rubber band, good old duct tape will work.

2. Take a strip of paper and fold it over and over until you have a small, tight square.

3. Place the folded piece of paper in between the chopsticks, directly under the rubber band. The paper will keep the chopsticks slightly apart. All you have to do is squeeze

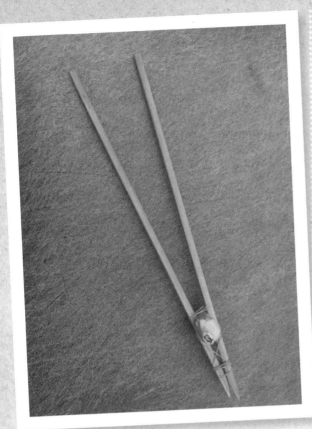

players think of a new category and the game starts again. The last person left is the winner!

The Spiderweb Game *(ages 5 and up)*
Can you be the first to untangle yourself from the spider's web?

Supplies: A ball of yarn or string for each player (preferably each in a different color)

1. To set up the game, each player needs a ball of yarn or string. It is best if each is a different color, but they don't have to be.
2. Tie or anchor securely the end of each ball of yarn to a different place: a tree, a picnic table, a rock, or other stationary object.
3. Unwind the yarn, taking it through obstacles, such as under a table, over a log, and around a tree.
4. Make it look like a spiderweb by overlapping your yarn with that of others.

them together to pinch things and pick them up.

Trivia Ball *(ages 6 and up)*
Think fast, and name that thing!

Supplies: A small, light ball like a tennis ball, a duct-tape ball, or a small rock

Players sit in a circle and decide on a category (animals, movies, books, colors, etc.). One person throws the ball to another player in the circle. That person has to immediately name an item in the category and throw the ball to someone else. If a player can't think of anything, or repeats something that's already been said, that player is out. The remaining

5. All the balls of yarn should meet at the end in one place; this is the players' starting point.

6. Players take the loose end of their yarn and make their way through the web, rewinding their ball of yarn.

The first player to untangle his yarn from the web wins.

Variation
Exchange the balls of yarn before rewinding.

Blindfold Shoe Shuffle *(ages 6 and up)*
Got some smelly hiking boots? That can be to your advantage in this group game!

Supplies:

- Blindfolds or bandanas (optional)
- Your shoes

Sit in a circle to start. Players put on a blindfold (or keep eyes shut) and take off their shoes. They then throw their shoes into a pile in the middle of the play area. The referee jumbles them all up (or places them randomly in a line) and then shouts "GO!" The first person to find his shoes by touch and smell alone and put them on is the winner. Though it's a race, you have to go carefully so you don't bonk heads. The referee needs to look out for this too.

What Am I? *(ages 7 and up)*
The answer is taped on your back, but you have to ask questions to figure out what you are in this game.

Supplies:

- Watch or stopwatch (optional)

- Tape
- Small pieces of paper or index cards
- Pens

Each player writes either an animal or a place on a card and tapes it to the back of another player without letting that person see what's on the card so that all players have one card stuck to their back. (You can pick a theme or category too.)

1. Stand in a circle and then pick somebody to step in the middle to guess what's on his card.

2. Tell the guesser if his card is a place or an animal.

3. The guesser has 30 seconds to ask as many yes-or-no questions he can about the place or animal on his card.

4. After the time is up, the guesser gets two more guesses.

5. Then it's the next person's turn to guess what's on her card. Go around until everyone has had a chance to guess.

Water Drop Race *(ages 4 and up)*
A race in miniature: Send that water moving toward the finish line with only your breath to power it.

Supplies:

- Sheet of aluminum foil (or waxed paper)
- Tape
- 2 straws (optional)

Tape your foil down onto a smooth surface. Put two drops of water at one end of the foil. Each player gets a straw. The first player to blow the drop of water across the length of the foil and off the edge wins.

It Was a Dark and Stormy Night . . .
(ages 7 and up)
Use props to make up a story around the campfire!

Supplies: 6 natural or camping objects

Gather half a dozen items, either from objects you have brought to camp or from your natural environment. Take turns making up ghost stories or other tall tales incorporating all the objects. You have to include them all somehow! As others tell their tales, they can use the same six things or a new set. Once you get the hang of it, you can even add a couple more objects.

> **Psst . . . Kids!** If you have younger siblings, be mindful about how spooky or creepy your story is. You don't want to ruin their camping experience. Besides, nightmares and crying kids affect the whole family, including you.

Game Inventor! *(ages 6 and up)*
Invent your own board game and challenge your friends and family!

Supplies:

- Paper
- Pen or pencil
- Pebbles or other small objects
- Scissors (optional)
- Crayons or colored pencils/pens (optional)
- Dice (optional)

Think of a **theme** for your game. There are two important features to make the game successful:

1. The players must have an **objective.**
2. There must be **obstacles** to achieving that objective.

Your theme could have to do with nature and camping or something else you know about, love, or imagine (sports, friendship, princesses or knights, school, animals, dinosaurs—you name it!). **Example:** The players could be bees. They have to stop on multiple flowers to gather pollen, watching out for spiders, birds, and badgers that want to eat them, and then have to return to the hive to make honey.

On your paper, plan your path. Mark the starting space and ending space, and then create the playing spaces in between. The path could go around the edges, zigzag, go in a spiral, or have multiple paths. Leave room to write inside the spaces. In some of the spaces, create obstacles or rewards. You could send a player forward one, two, or three spaces or send them back one, two, or three spaces. It is more fun if there is a reason, such as *Chased by a hungry bird. Go back three spaces.* Decorate your game board.

Collect pebbles or acorns for game pieces. If you don't have dice, you can use playing cards to determine how many spaces you can move. Or on another piece of paper, divide it into four or six spaces. Players can roll or toss a pebble onto the paper to determine how far they can move. You can also make cards with instructions and create spaces that say "Take a card."

Invite your fellow campers to play your game! Remember, if you don't like how the game works the first time, you can always change or improve it for the next round.

Variations

- Decorate your board with actual rocks or leaves and other woodland debris as obstacles, using mud glue. (See page 166.)
- Some of the spaces or instruction cards could command the players to do actions, such as *Bark like a dog!*

It Just Takes People Games

All you need to play these games is enthusiasm. That makes these mostly verbal games great for on the trail or around the campfire.

Left, Right, Still *(ages 5 and up)*

This game is similar to Simon Says but has a fun and challenging twist. The Caller comes up with three words that start with the same first letter sound. For instance: tent, tree, and turtle. The Caller then clarifies the rules for the three words. For example:

- When the Caller calls "tent," everyone has to step to the right.

- When the Caller calls "tree," everyone has to step to the left.
- When the Caller calls "turtle," everyone has to stand still.

The Caller starts calling out the three words. Any player who steps the wrong way is out. The last person left playing is the winner and becomes the Caller.

Variation

Allow the Caller to change the movements as well as the three words. For example, the new words and movements might be:

- Cat: Kick your leg out.
- Crow: Squat down.
- Cake: Turn in a circle.

Freeze Dance *(ages 2 and up)*

Sing a song or put on some tunes and get ready to boogie and freeze.

One person can play the music and judge, or you can have two people play these roles. Whenever the music stops, you must freeze. Don't be the last person moving when the music stops. The judge can also call out/award the craziest, most creative, most rhythmic, most cool, most professional dance, or whatever category you can come up with.

Variation

Freeze Brush. Put some fun into brushing your teeth in the camp bathroom or over the water spigot. One person hums a tune, and everyone dances in place while you brush. Take turns saying "Freeze!" Freeze in whatever position you are in for 3 seconds then continue brushing. This is a great way to get in your 2 full minutes of brushing and have it go by fast.

Poor Kitty! *(ages 3 and up)*
A purr-fect game for getting the giggles! Try not to laugh!

Pick one person to be the "kitty." That person has to go up to a player and act like a kitten (meowing, purring, etc.). The player has to pat the *kitty* on the head three times and say "Poor kitty" WITHOUT LAUGHING! Yes, you must keep a straight face. If the player is successful at not laughing, the kitty moves on to a different person. If not, the person who laughed becomes the kitty!

Buzz! *(ages 8 and up)*
1-2-3-4-5-6-Buzz! Whatever you do, don't say the number . . . Buzz!

Take turns counting numbers. When you get to a number that is either a multiple of 7 or contains the number 7, you must say "Buzz" instead of the number. You can play this as a cooperative or competitive game. If cooperative, just see how far you can count. If someone says a Buzz number, like 21 or 47, instead of "Buzz," others can yell out "Buzz" and you keep going. Or you can play that the whole group has to start over again.

As a competitive game, you can play it as an elimination game: If someone says a number when he should say "Buzz," he is out and play continues. Or you can play for points: Each time a player misses a Buzz or waits too long before saying either "Buzz" or the number, or if a person says "Buzz" when it isn't a Buzz, she gets a letter and is out when she spells B-U-Z-Z.

Variation
Try it with another number instead of 7.

Backwards Alphabet Race *(ages 8 and up)*
Z-Y-X-W-Oh, man! What comes next? See if you can recite the alphabet backward and quicker than anyone else.

You can do this one as an individual challenge, racing against the clock, or in teams, racing against one another. If playing in teams, teammates take turns saying the next letter. The first team to finish could have to run and touch a tree or do something else to make it easier for the person judging the race.

The 21 Game *(ages 8 and up)*
Players take turns saying a number. The first player says "1," and each player in turn increases the number by 1, 2, or 3, but may not exceed 21. The player forced to say "21" loses.

The 100 Game *(ages 9 and up)*
Who will be the first to say "100" and win the game?

Two players start from 0 and alternatively add a number from 1 to 10 to the sum. The player who reaches 100 wins.

Bulls & Cows *(ages 8 and up)*
No cattle on the trail? Well now there are with the game Bulls & Cows! Players take turns trying to guess one another's number. You can play it with or without a pen and paper. This game can be played in teams of guessers.

1. The chooser thinks of a four-digit number. All digits must be different.

2. The guesser tries to guess the number by naming a four-digit number.

3. The chooser says how close the guess is to the answer by telling the guesser:

   - The number of Bulls: digits correct in the right position.

   - The number of Cows: digits correct but in the wrong position.

4. The guesser tries to guess the answer in the fewest number of turns.

Example:
If the chooser has thought of the number 2,745, the replies for some guesses are as follows:

- Guess: 1,389; reply: 0 Bulls, 0 Cows

- Guess: 1,234; reply: 0 Bulls, 2 Cows

- Guess: 1,759; reply: 1 Bull, 1 Cow

- Guess: 1,785; reply: 2 Bulls, 0 Cows

- Guess: 2,745; reply: 4 Bulls!

Variations

- **Word Bulls & Cows.** Choose and guess words instead of numbers. It's really fun!

- Play with three- or five-digit numbers or three- or five-letter words.

- **Fermi, Pico, Bagel** is a great variation that can also be played with any number of digits. The chooser gives these clues to the guesser: Fermi is the right number in the right place. Pico is the right number in the wrong place. Bagel is a wrong number. For example, if the correct number was 831, and the guesser suggests the number 981, the chooser would say: Bagel, Pico, Fermi. The

guesser knows 8 is in the number, but in the wrong place, 3 is not in the number, and 1 is correct and in the right place. Guessing continues until the right answer is achieved.

Did You Know?
The commercial game Mastermind is based on Bulls & Cows!

Bonus Problem: What is the minimum number of guesses needed that will allow you to always determine a secret number when the secret number has one digit? When the secret number has two digits? When the secret number has three digits?

Psst . . . Kids! It's okay to write down the number on a piece of paper if that makes it easier.

Going on a Campout *(ages 7 and up)*
You have to guess what you can bring and can't bring to this camping trip in this guessing game in which players try to guess the Leader's Secret Rule!

1. One person is the Leader and thinks of a rule for what can be brought to camp. For instance, people can only bring items beginning with the letter S, like salad or salami. Or people can only bring items that have three letters, like cup and dog. Or the items can only be vegetables.

2. The Leader starts, saying, "I'm going on a campout and bringing a ____." She finishes this phrase with a word that follows the rule.

3. Players take turns suggesting items to bring on the campout. "I'm going on the campout and bringing a ____."

4. If the suggestion follows the rule, the Leader tells the player he can come on the campout. If the suggestion doesn't follow the rule, the Leader tells the player he can't come on the campout.

5. If players think they've figured out the rule, they can guess it on their turn. The player who guesses correctly becomes the new Leader.

Portmanteau Play *(ages 6 and up)*

Make up your own descriptions of what you see along the trail or around camp by creating portmanteaus (pawrt-MAN-tohs).

Did You Know?

The Dope on Portmanteaus

The author Lewis Carroll introduced portmanteau words in his book *Through the Looking-Glass* in 1871 in the poem "Jabberwocky." Humpty Dumpty explains to Alice: "You see it's like a portmanteau—there are two meanings packed up into one word." In "Jabberwocky," *Slithy* means "lithe and slimy" and *mimsy* is "flimsy and miserable." By definition, a portmanteau is a large suitcase that opens into two equal sections.

A **portmanteau word** is made by combining two (or more) words or their sounds and meanings to make a new single word. A few commonly used portmanteaus are *smog* (smoke and fog), *motel* (motor and hotel), and *brunch* (breakfast and lunch). You can also call something *prettiful* (pretty and beautiful) or *orruglible* (ugly and horrible).

Take turns making up portmanteau words to describe what you see along the trail. For variations, make adjectives (descriptive words), nouns (things, places, persons, concepts), and verbs (actions). See if others can guess the two words that make up your portmanteau.

That's Punny! *(ages 8 and up)*

Get campy at camp, and play with puns! A pun is a play on words created by using words in a sentence so that they can have more than one meaning. Some puns will make you laugh. Some will make you cringe. But making them up is really fun. *Warning:* Punning can be contagious!

Here are a few jokes featuring puns. The objects being punned are in italics. The punch lines are in bold.

- Did you hear about the guy whose *whole left side* was cut off? He's **all right** now.

- To write with a *broken pencil* is **pointless**.

- I'm reading a book about *antigravity*. It's **impossible to put down**.

- I'm glad I know *sign language*; it's pretty **handy**.

- *A bicycle* can't stand on its own because it is **two-tired**.

- Why are *teddy bears* never hungry? They are always **stuffed**!
- Why did the *spider* go to the computer? To check his **web**site.

You can play That's Punny! while hiking or resting in camp or at the beach or anywhere. Look around you and see how many puns you can come up with the objects around you.

Example:

- Player #1 says, "Being in the forest is a big tree-t."
- Player #2 says, "This looks like a good place to branch out my education."

Tongue Twister Time *(ages 6 and up)*

Say this five times fast: She sells seashells at the seashore. Tongue twisters use alliteration—the repetition of the same initial letter, sound, or group of sounds in a series of words. It's really fun to make up your own. Or try out a few of these classics. How many times and how fast can you say them?

> *Peter Piper picked a peck of pickled peppers.*
> *A peck of pickled peppers, Peter Piper picked.*
> *If Peter Piper picked a peck of pickled peppers,*
> *Where's the peck of pickled peppers Peter Piper picked?*

Flash message. Flash message.

A proper copper coffeepot.

Other Wordplay Games *(ages 6 and up)*

Having language to play with is like having a full toy box. These games are great on the trail or around the campfire.

Positively Opposites. Younger campers might enjoy a game of opposites (antonyms) on the trail. Challenge them to name a word opposite in meaning to the word you say: good–bad; up–down.

The Same Game. Little and big kids might enjoy the challenge of coming up with synonyms. A synonym is a word having the same or nearly the same meaning as another. Suggest a word, such as *big*, and have campers come up with words and phrases that mean the same, like *huge* and *large*.

Sounds Abound in Words. *Pow! Wham!* Name or make up as many onomatopoeias as you can or make up ones that describe a certain situation. Onomatopoeias describe or imitate a natural sound or the sound made by an object or an action.

Exaggeration Nation. An exaggeration that is so dramatic that no one would believe the statement is true is called a hyperbole. Tall tales are hyperboles. Start with a statement like "I am so hungry . . ." and use hyperbole to tell the tale: "I am so hungry, I could eat a pine tree."

Expression Impression. Every language or culture has expressions particular to culture. We call these idioms. They have a figurative meaning often quite different from the literal meaning. **Examples:** "You're pulling my leg!" "I'm keeping an eye on you!" There are an estimated 25,000 idioms in the English language, with more coming into our language every day. Idioms are the hardest thing for a second-language speaker to learn. Name as

Family Conversation Starters

- What is usually your first thought when you wake up?
- What is your most cherished item?
- What are the three most interesting things about you?
- If you could have a conversation with anyone in history, who would it be? What would you ask that person?
- What is your earliest memory?
- If you could change the world, what would you change?
- If you could change one thing about your appearance, what would it be?
- What is your idea of an ideal day?

many idioms as you can, and describe what the literal meaning would look like.

Clapping Games

Keep the rhythm,
Clap your hands everyone,
'Cause these clapping games
Are a lot of fun!

My New Tent *(ages 8 and up)*

Find the right word to describe your new tent, but do it with rhythm.

1. Players sit in a circle on the ground or around the picnic table.

2. The first player describes the new tent with a word that begins with the letter A. So that

player might say, "My new tent is an Awesome tent."

3. The next person uses a word that begins with B: "My new tent is a Big tent."

4. Go around the circle, making your way through the alphabet.

5. One catch: You have to keep a rhythm going as you play! Make the rhythm by slapping your knees twice and clapping your hands twice.

6. A player who can't think of a word that starts with the right letter to describe the tent is out.

7. The remaining players continue the game, picking up at the letter where the last person left off.

8. Keep playing until one player is left.

Variation

With younger campers, do the game without the rhythmic time constraint or do it more slowly.

Slap Clap

Slap, slap, clap, clap! Say someone's name in the circle, and keep the rhythm going!

1. Players sit in a circle and set a rhythm by slapping their knees twice and clapping their hands twice.

2. The first player says his name twice on the knee slaps and another player's name twice on the hand claps.

3. The player who is named must continue the game in the same way.

4. If a player is off beat, or messes up, she's out!

5. Keep playing until there's only one person left.

Rhythm Leader *(ages 5 and up)*

It starts like Slap Clap, but in this game you have to keep up with a new rhythm all the time.

1. Players sit in a circle and set a rhythm by slapping their knees twice and clapping their hands twice.

2. The first player says his name twice on the knee slaps and another player's name twice on the hand claps.

3. When you say another player's name, that player starts a new rhythm combination. (**Example:** snap clap, snap slap.) Everyone else imitates her. When everyone gets it, she says her name in the first part of the rhythm and another player's name in the second part of the rhythm.

4. That player then has to create a new rhythm combination and the game continues.

Variations

- Try to make the rhythm more complicated as you go. Add mouth sounds and dance moves!

- Try Rhythm Leader *without* saying names. One person starts by creating any rhythm, and everyone else joins in. After you've got a beat going for a while, without saying anything, another player takes the lead, changing something in the rhythm to make it new. When everyone has got that one down, a different player takes the lead, changing something in the rhythm, and everyone else must follow.

Who Took the Cookies from the Cookie Jar? *(ages 3 and up)*

In this rhythmic clapping and rhyming game, name names and try to keep it going!

1. Sit around a picnic table or in a circle on the ground.

2. Start a clapping rhythm of two slaps on the table or on your thighs and two claps.

3. One player starts out and chants to the rhythm. In the second line, that player says someone's name in the circle.

Who took the cookies from the cookie jar?
[Name] took the cookies from the cookie jar.
The person just named says:
Who me?
Everyone in the circle responds:
Yes, you!
The person named says:
Couldn't be.
Everyone answers:
Then who?

4. The person named names someone else in the circle, and the game continues, with that person responding:

[Name] took the cookies from the cookie jar!

Here is the rhyme in its entirety:

Who took the cookie from the cookie jar?
[Name] took the cookie from the cookie jar.
Who me?
Yes, you!
Couldn't be!
Then who?

[Name] took the cookie from the cookie
jar.
Who me?
Yes, you!
Couldn't be!
Then who?
[Name] took the cookie from the cookie
jar.

Variations

- If playing as an elimination game, players are eliminated by failing to keep up with the prescribed beat.
- After one round with everyone's name, try speeding up the tempo. Keep making it faster.
- Try using claps, snaps, and foot stomps in different combinations. A round leader can decide on a new combination.

I Woke Up Saturday Morning
(ages 6 and up)

Be ready! In this circle clapping game, when you get to the end of the folk rhyme, clap another hand and not your own or you're out!

1. Players sit in a circle and put both hands out in front of them with palms facing up.
2. Overlap hands so your right hand is above the left hand of the person sitting on your right. One person starts by reaching over with his right hand and clapping the right hand of the person sitting on their left.
3. The clap is passed around the circle while the group says this rhyme:

I woke up Saturday morning
I looked up on the wall

I saw a team of roaches
playing basketball.
The score was 10 to nothing
the roaches in the lead
I got a can of bug spray, one, two three!

- If a player's hand is clapped on "three," that player is out.
- If the player pulls her hand away in time and the person claps his own hand, then that person is out.
- When there are only two people left in the game, the hand positions change. Player 1 holds both hands out, palms facing up. Player #2 slaps Player #1's hands with both of his hands, palms facing down. Now, Player #2 holds her hands out and Player #1 slaps her hands.
- Play continues until there is only one person left!

One Frog in the Water

In this clapping rhythm game, if you can't keep the beat, you go *kerplunk*.

1. Players sit in a circle.
2. The first person says "One Frog."
3. The next person says "In the water."
4. And the next person says *"Kerplunk."*
5. Now, increase everything by one.
6. So the next person in the circle says "Two Frogs."
7. And the next person says "Two Frogs."
8. The person after that says "In the water."
9. And the next person says "In the water."
10. The person after that says *"Kerplunk."*

11. And the next person says "*Kerplunk*."

12. Keep going around the circle, increasing everything by one.

13. But there's one catch: All players have to slap their knees and clap, keeping the rhythm while the game goes around the circle.

14. If a player is off the beat, hesitates, or says the wrong thing, he's out.

15. Continue the game until there is only one person left.

Chase and Tag Games

All tag and chase games require two or more players. (They get more fun with more players.)

Rope Tag *(ages 3 and up)*

Don't let that rope get you, and be ready to jump!

Supplies: At least a 5-foot piece of rope

1. Pick one person to spin the rope. Everyone else gets in a circle around him.

2. The rope holder spins the rope low to the ground.

3. Everyone else tries to jump over the rope.

4. The rope should spin fast enough that it doesn't hit the ground, but slow enough that it's not going too fast for people to jump over.

5. If a person gets tagged by the rope, he is out.

6. The last person not tagged by the rope is the winner.

Duck, Duck, Goose *(ages 2 and up)*

This classic chase and tag game can be honkin' fun with the family, engaging campers of all ages.

1. Players sit in a circle in camp chairs or on a patch of grass, facing inward.

2. One player becomes the Picker and walks around tapping on each player's head or shoulder, calling each a Duck until finally picking one to be a Goose.

3. The Goose then rises and chases the Picker, trying to tag her while the Picker tries to return to and sit where the Goose had been sitting.

4. If the Picker succeeds, the Goose becomes the Picker and a new round begins.

5. If the Goose succeeds in tagging the Picker, the Goose may return to sit in the previous spot and the Picker remains the Picker for another round.

Variations

- **Mush Pot.** If the Picker is tagged, she has to sit in the center of the circle, in the Mush Pot, until another person is tagged and she is replaced.

- **Duck Duck Splash.** Playing on the beach on a hot day? The Picker carries a small bucket of water and uses it to splash the Goose.

- **Duck Duck Animal.** Choose another animal instead of a goose to represent the person who is *it*. He could be an amoeba, a rhinoceros, or a horse. To add a twist, the Picker is the Duck and has to quack and flap his wings as he makes his way around the circle, while the chaser has to make the chosen animal sounds and movements.

Ounch, Neech (or Up, Down)
(ages 5 and up)

This tag game comes from Pakistan and is perfect in the outdoors because you need lots of obstacles in your playing field, like tree stumps, logs, and rocks. You can also use the picnic bench and camp chairs.

1. One person is *it*. He calls out either "ounch (up)" or "neech (down)."

2. If he chooses "neech (down)," then the ground is not safe. Players can be tagged out unless they are up on something like a stump or a rock.

3. The opposite is true as well: If *it* chooses "ounch (up)," then the ground is safe, so everyone remains with feet on the ground.

4. Players try to risk it, being down when *it* says "up" and up when *it* says "down" in order to get to a free base.

5. The first person tagged becomes *it* for the next round of the game.

Variation
Create a time limit, such as 3 seconds, in which players can stay on the same object before having to find another.

Pilolo *(ages 4 and up)*
This game comes from rural Ghana in West Africa, where toys are often quite limited, but they find plenty of ways to have fun, like playing Pilolo.

Supplies: Marked stick, rock, or pinecone

1. Use nontoxic paint or pens or duct tape to mark up a stick, rock, or pinecone (so it is distinguishable from others in the area).

2. One person becomes the Leader.

3. The Leader or another person acts as Timekeeper.

4. Determine boundaries for your play area, and create a finish line.

5. Players turn their backs while the Leader secretly hides the marked stick, rock, or pinecone.

6. The Timekeeper (or Leader/Timekeeper) waits at the finish line to judge which player is first.

7. When the Leader says "Pilolo!" (which means "time to search for") the Timekeeper starts the watch and players race to be the first to find the hidden item and take it across the finish line.

8. The winner is awarded 1 point.

9. The game is repeated as many times as you wish.

10. The player with the most points wins.

Variation

Add an obstacle course to the playing field that each player must go through to get to the finish line.

Decomposing! *(ages 5 and up)*

Help your fellow players before they completely decompose in this group tag game.

1. To play, pick someone to be *it*. That player runs around and tries to tag the other players.

2. When someone is tagged, he starts to "decompose." (It works best if you count to 10 slowly while you fall to the ground.)

3. Someone who's not *it* has to tap the tagged person again before she decomposes all the way down to the ground. When tapped, the decomposing player can run around again.

4. The first person to decompose all the way to the ground is *it* during the next round.

Did You Know?

The Dirt on Decomposition

Decomposition is an extremely vital ecological process. It breaks down organisms into simple molecules like carbon dioxide and water. It recycles nutrients back to the soil. Earthworms, insects, and snails are examples of animals that help decompose what was once living matter.

Stuck in the Mud *(ages 5 and up)*

You might get stuck, but you won't get muddy in this game of tag.

1. When the person who is *it* tags someone, he is stuck in the mud and can't move.

2. To get unstuck, someone else has to crawl through his legs.

3. Players help one another out of the sticky mud. If everybody gets tagged, the game is over.

4. The last person to be tagged is *it* in the next round.

Variation

To make it harder, or if you have more people, you can add this twist: If a player touches the stuck player's legs when crawling through them, he is stuck too.

Kick the Can *(ages 6 and up)*

This classic combines hide-and-seek and tag.

Supplies: An old soda or beer can, tin can, cup, or bucket

1. One person is *it.* That person starts out guarding the can.
2. *It* closes her eyes and counts to some high number while everyone else hides.
3. When *it* reaches the designated number, she runs around to find everybody.

4. The tricky part: Once a person is found, he has to race to kick the can over before *it* tags him.
5. If the person found kicks the can first, *it* has to look for other players.
6. If *it* tags the person first, the round is over and the tagged person is *it.* The rest of the players come back to the start.

Catch 'Em by the Tail *(ages 5 and up)*

Catch others by their tails, but don't let them grab yours!

Supplies: Socks

1. To play, you need one sock for every player.
2. First, players hang their sock from their back pocket or waistband. (This is their "tail.")
3. On the word *go*, players try to take other players' tails without letting anyone else get theirs.
4. When a player's tail is taken or falls off, she has to sit down. Even though she's sitting, she's not out. She can grab the tail off of anybody who runs by. If she gets somebody's tail, she can hang it from her back pocket and start running around again.
5. The last player standing wins.

Racing Games

When you want to get the blood pumping and play around camp or on the lakeshore, get racing!

Carry On If You Can! *(ages 4 and up)*

This game, using only a small rock, has eight or more fun challenges to master in order to win. Play on your own, against others, or in teams. It's great for balance and coordination too.

Supplies: Rocks (smooth rocks about the size of your palm, rather flat)

1. Find two game rocks for each player.
2. Clear a space in the dirt or grass about 15 or 20 feet in length, depending on the age of your players. Make it longer if you want more of a challenge.
3. Draw lines with a stick for your starting and finish lines.
4. If at any time you fall over or drop a rock in a round, you have to start that round again.
5. The first player to get through all rounds wins. (Or keep times, and the best time wins.)

Round 1: Toss one rock. Toss your second rock so it hits the first. Pick up both rocks. Toss the target rock again and try to hit it with your other rock. Continue to the finish line.

Round 2: Toss your rock, hop twice until you reach it, pick it up while still on one foot, and repeat to the finish line. (You can create more rounds with more hops.)

Round 3: Balance the rock on the top of your foot and hop toward and over the finish line without dropping it.

Round 4: Put the rock between your feet and hop to the finish line without dropping the rock. (You can do a round with the rock between your knees, thighs, or elbows too!)

Round 5: Put the rock on your chest and either crab walk or walk limbo style to the finish line without dropping the rock.

Round 6: Put the rock between your chin and chest and hold it in place with no hands while you walk to the finish line.

Round 7: Put the rock on your right shoulder and hold it there with your cheek and ear (but no hands) and walk to the finish line. (Do the same on your left shoulder.)

Round 8: Put the rock between your feet, turn around, and jump backward to the finish line. (Do the same between your knees, thighs, or elbows.)

Variations

- Make up your own rounds and add more to make it a longer game, or take turns among players deciding on each round. You can change things up each time you play.
- Make a race out of any one of these, such as the rock between your knees!
- Get a bunch of rocks, and move as many as you can to drop them in a container or bucket at the finish line. Catch: You can only carry the rocks on your feet, or any other way the players choose.
- What else can you put on your foot to race with? What about a handkerchief?

Obstacle Course *(ages 2 and up)*

You can create an infinite number of obstacle courses out in nature! Create your own course around the campground or wherever you might be hanging out for a while.

Example:

- Start at the stump, jump over that log, run a circle around that tree, touch that boulder, go around the ferns, hug the sapling, and run back and touch the stump.

- Time how fast you can complete the course, or have two or more people race.

- The winner can change the obstacle course or even add a goofy command, such as "Stand on that rock and hoot like an owl."

Pancake Flip Relay *(ages 6 and up)*

What better way to top off a camping breakfast than a pancake flip relay!

Supplies:

- 1 or 2 lightweight frying pans

- Leftover pancakes or something representing a pancake, like a plastic container lid; or make a duct-tape disc.

1. Divide players into two teams.
2. Decide your start and finish lines.
3. Walk as quickly as you can to a finish line and back.
4. With each step, flip the pancake (or imitation pancake) and catch it in the frying pan.
5. Then pass the frying pan and pancake to the next person on your team so that he can do the same thing.
6. First team to finish wins.
7. If you've only got one frying pan, time your teams. The team with the best time wins. Consider giving the runner-up team a chance to beat the winning time.

Rock, Tree, Tent Race *(ages 4 and up)*

Rock, tent, or tree—be one of the three in this racing game that's best for three or more players.

1. Decide on a start and finish line.
2. Set a timer and go!
3. The first person in line is the Rock. She ducks down on her knees with her head tucked in.
4. The second person in line jumps over the Rock and stands up to become the Tree.
5. The third person in line jumps over the Rock, goes around the Tree twice, and makes a two-door Tent with his body by putting hands and feet on the ground while keeping his midsection in the air.
6. The person who was the Rock then goes around the Tree two times, goes through the Tent, and becomes a Rock again.
7. Keep repeating this pattern until you reach the finish line.
8. Switch positions and try again to get the fastest time.

Other Racing Games

Here are some other types of races you can try!

- **Jumping Race.** To win this race, you don't have to be the first to finish, you have to finish in the least number of jumps.

- **Two Forward, One Back.** Each player has to hop (both legs together) two jumps forward, then one jump back, to the finish line.

- **Make up your own!**

Tent Games

Rain doesn't have to ruin your camping fun. Here are some games you can play in your tent. Leave your shoes outside, and bring in the fun!

Footsie *(ages 3 and up)*

Get ready to grab the ball . . . with your feet!

Supplies: A rolled-up pair of socks, a plastic cup, a duct-tape ball, or a tennis ball

1. Players lie down and put their legs in the air.
2. One player puts a ball between her feet and passes it to the next player.

3. Try to get the ball all the way around the circle.
4. Try to pass it faster.

Variations

- Pretend the ball is a stink bomb. If someone drops it, imagine everyone gets skunked out.
- Play this as an elimination game. If a player drops the ball, he's out. Keep doing this until all the players but one is out.
- Play as a Footie Hot Potato. One person sings or plays music while the others pass the ball. The person with the ball when the music stops is out or gets a letter in the word *footie*. If the person drops the ball to the floor to avoid it, she gets two letters.

Ha, Ha *(ages 4 and up)*

Try not to laugh in this game that is no laughing matter!

1. Players lie down on their backs so that each player's head rests on another player's stomach.
2. One player begins by saying "Ha."
3. The next player says, "Ha, Ha."
4. Each player adds another "Ha" when it's his turn.
5. The object is to say "Ha" as many times as you can without anybody giggling. If someone giggles, you have to start back at one "Ha" again. How ha-high can you go?

Skillful Toes *(ages 3 and up)*

Show off your toe finesse in this barefoot game.

Supplies:

- Coins or small, smooth, flat river rocks the size of coins (wash them off!)
- Plates for each player plus one more

1. Take off your socks and bare your feet!
2. Put your game pieces on a plate in the middle of the players.
3. Each player should also have an empty plate.
4. Players have 60 seconds to grab as many coins from the pile as they can and transfer them to their empty plate. *But they can only use the toes on one foot.*
5. At the end of 60 seconds, players add up all the change on their plate. The player with the most money wins!
6. Now try it with the other foot.

Horse Sock Basketball *(ages 2 and up)*

You can still play a rousing game of Horse Basketball, even in a tent. The smaller the tent, the more clever or strange your shots have to be to stump the other players.

Supplies:

- Socks
- A pot, bucket, or stiff bag that will stay open

1. Roll socks together into balls.
2. Take turns trying to shoot the socks into the pot "hoop."
3. Each player has to shoot like the first player.
4. The first player can shoot anyway he wants. It could be sitting cross-legged across the tent, on his knees, or backward over his shoulder. He can shoot it while rolling on his back. Or with eyes shut. Or launching it with his feet. Whatever he comes up with! But he can't stand up.

5. When a player misses the shot, she gets the letter H.

6. If the person who decided the shot makes it, he gets to decide the next one. If he misses, the lead goes to the next player.

7. Players who get all the letters to spell H-O-R-S-E are out. When all players are eliminated but one, the last person is the winner.

Sleeping Bag Tidal Wave *(ages 3 and up)*

This game is also great to play when folding laundry as a family at home.

Supplies:

- Rolled-up socks in different colors
- Sleeping bag or sheet or blanket

1. Roll up a different colored pair of socks for each player.

2. Get on either side of a sleeping bag, the long way.

3. Put your socks on top of the sleeping bag, in the middle.

4. Holding the sleeping bag by its corners, together lift it off the floor.

5. On "Go," shake the bag to try to knock your opponent's socks off while yours stay on.

6. The last player with her socks on the bag is the winner.

7. With four players, you can open up the bag to make it bigger. Or try the game on a sheet or blanket, with each player holding a corner.

Not on My Side! *(ages 2 and up)*

A frenetic game with socks that will make you smile!

Supplies:

- Balled-up socks
- Timer (optional)

1. Divide the space in the tent in half, using sleeping bags and clothes bags as a divider in the middle.

2. Ball up as many pairs of socks as possible, and start with an equal number on each side.

3. Players sit on either side of the divide and on "go" start throwing socks into the other team's area. Players have to remain seated.

4. If you have a timer, set it for 1 minute. When the time is up, the side with fewer socks wins. (Put everything back where you found it when you're done!)

Other In-Tent Activities:

- Read books and magazines
- Read aloud to each other
- Card games
- Board games
- Crafting (knitting, sewing, drawing)
- Make up stories to tell one another
- Sing songs
- Listen to music on a portable device
- Watch movies on a portable device
- Snuggle

Night Games

Play these games when the sun goes down for a little nighttime fun.

Glow-in-the-Dark Bowling *(ages 2 and up)*

Put light sticks into 2-liter bottles or 16-ounce water bottles. Use a ball or rock to try to knock them down.

Shadow Puppets *(ages 2 and up)*

With a light source nearby, you can make shadows against the side of your tent. Try using your hands and body to make different shadows. Can you make a wolf? A duck? A spider? A butterfly?

Hide and Go *Beep* *(ages 4 and up)*

When it's dark, play a variation on hide-and-seek. Find a space where players won't trip or run into unseen objects. Locate one another by sound. Hidden players must go *beep* every 30 seconds or so.

Flashlight Tag *(ages 6 and up)*

You just need a flashlight for this great combination of tag and hide-and-seek that makes the dark more fun.

The person who is *it* (the Seeker) has a flashlight and counts to at least 30 at base. Everyone else hides. The Seeker then looks for people. To tag someone, the Seeker must shine the light on that person and call out his name. That person becomes the Seeker and takes the flashlight; the game starts again.

Variation

Group Flashlight Tag. Everyone has a flashlight. Count up to 60 to allow everyone to hide. Players try to tag other players by finding them and shining a flashlight on them. Tagged players are then out. Play until only one person remains.

Psst . . . Kids! Because it's dark, don't let anyone go too long before being found or having everyone come back to base. Be careful not to shine the light in people's eyes after you find them!

Signals *(ages 7 and up)*

Players pair off and create their own flashlight signal (three short flashes, two long and one short flash, etc.). Partners then separate and go to opposite ends of a large, open playing area. Players are given 1 minute to scatter before they begin flashing their signals. Each pair tries to reunite as quickly as possible by sending flashlight signals to their partners. The first pair to reunite is the winner.

Family Constellations *(ages 5 and up)*

On a clear night, lie on your back and look up into the sky. Pretend that you have been given the task of finding and naming constellations for your family and friends. Find at least three constellations of your own making and describe what you see and how to locate them. Make up a legend for fellow stargazers.

Ghost Stories *(ages 8 and up)*

There are many classic ghost stories. Make sure your kids are okay with scary or gross stories before telling them. This can be especially fun for older kids. Consider putting younger kids to bed first and letting older ones stay up a little later for this, if you think they will enjoy it and be able to sleep afterward. If you don't know any classic ghost stories, make something up (see It Was a Dark and Stormy Night game, page 131), search online, or check out books from your public library.

Paper & Pencil Games

These games require only paper and a pen or pencil. You don't have to haul in bulky boxed board games to have a variety of challenging and fun games to play while camping. Paper-and-pencil games are great to play at the picnic table while relaxing around camp. If a camper needs a break from all the activity and stimuli of the outdoors, these games are the ticket! They also serve as a wonderful way for family members to interact one-on-one. Especially between older kids and their parents, when does that happen in our daily lives?

Things I Love *(ages 6 and up)*

Learn more about what your family members love.

Supplies: Paper and pencils/pens

Give all members of your family a heart cut out of paper and have them write down their favorite color, movie, book, animal, and food. Add any other categories the group agrees on. Then put all the hearts into a hat and have people take turns reading them. Try to guess who you think the author of each heart is. You can go an extra step and have people explain why they love that item.

I Never *(ages 7 and up)*

Never say *never* in this group game that lets you get to know your fellow campers better.

Supplies: Paper and pencils/pens

1. Cut or tear up paper into smaller slips.
2. Campers think of something they have done, might have done, or think somebody else might've done and write it down on a slip of paper. **Example:** If the comment is "slept in until 1 p.m.," write, "I've never slept in until 1 p.m."
3. Write on as many slips as you wish. The more things each person writes, the longer the game takes to play.
4. Put the slips of paper face down on the table in the center of the group or in a container that you can pass around.
5. Take turns reading the slips.
6. If someone has done the thing written on the slip, such as slept in until 1 p.m., he has to raise his hand. If the person reading the slip has done the thing written on it, she has to raise her hand too.
7. When they raise their hands, players then talk about the wacky things they've done.

Truth or Lie *(ages 8 and up)*

Try to fool your fellow campers with a lie that sounds like a fact about you.

Players write two true things and one false thing about themselves on their paper. Take turns reading them aloud, or pass them around (with your name on it).

The other players have to try to guess what's not true.

Variation

Write four true things and one false thing.

Word Countdown *(ages 10 and up)*

This fun word game gets its name from the British TV game show *Countdown,* one of the longest-running TV game shows in history (from 1982 to present, with over 6,000 episodes). How long a word can you create from randomly chosen letters? The longest word from a set of nine letters is the winner.

1. Players take turns choosing letters until nine letters have been named and written down.
2. Each player tries to construct a word using just those letters.
3. The player who has found the longest word scores 1 point per letter, double for a nine-letter word. In the case of a draw, both players score.

Example:
If the players chose the letters A-W-Y-R-E-B-S-T-D, they might find BEAST, DRAWER, and STRAYED, with STRAYED being the winner and scoring 7 points.

Variations

- The game can be played with any number of letters; eight, nine, or ten letters work.
- Include a "?" as a wildcard, which players can use as any letter they wish.
- Set different time limits.

Number Countdown (ages 8 and up)
This game is also from the TV game show *Countdown.* Be a math whiz! Compete to reach a target total by combining six numbers using arithmetic.

1. One player secretly writes two large numbers (25, 50, 75, or 100) and four small numbers (from 1 to 10) on a piece of paper.
2. The other player secretly writes a three-digit target.
3. After revealing the numbers and target, players have to try to get as near to the target as possible by combining some or all of the six numbers using addition, subtraction, multiplication, and division. Only integers (whole numbers, no fractions) may be used at any stage in the calculation, and you can only use each number once.
4. The player who gets closest to the target scores 10 points for getting the target exactly, 7 points for getting within 5 of the target, or 5 points for getting within 10 of the target. If both players are equally close, they both score. No points are scored for an answer more than 10 from the target.

Example:

- Player #1 secretly selects the numbers 75, 50, 2, 3, 8, and 7.
- Player #2 secretly selects 812 as the target number.
- Player #1 gets to 813 with the following math: $75 + 50 - 8 = 117$, and $117 \times 7 - (3 \times 2) = 813$, which scores 7 points.

Variations

- Set different time limits. On the TV game show *Countdown,* contestants have 30 seconds.
- For each round when less than 10 is scored, work together to figure out how to achieve the target number exactly.

Dots and Boxes (ages 8 and up)
This game of strategy is known by many names: Boxes, Squares, Paddocks, Pigs in a Pen, Square-it, Dots and Dashes, Dots, Line Game, Smart Dots, Dot Boxing, or, simply, the Dot Game. Whatever you call it, it's fun! Take

turns drawing lines between dots on a grid. The player who completes the most boxes wins. (This game dates back to 1889.)

1. Draw a three × three grid of dots, nine dots total.

2. Take turns drawing vertical or horizontal lines between two adjacent dots to connect them.

3. Players who complete the fourth side of a box initial that box and must draw another line.

4. When all the boxes have been completed, the winner is the player who has initialed the most boxes.

5. Even a four × four grid can be challenging and require skill.

Variations
You can play with three × three, four × four, five × four, five × five, or six × four squares. Three × three is good for beginners, five × five for experts.

Domineering (ages 8 and up)
This relative of Dots and Boxes is also known as Crosscram or Stop-Gate. Get ready to domineer! Take turns linking pairs of dots on a grid. The first player unable to move loses.

1. The game is played on a matrix of dots. Start with five × five.

2. Players take turns linking a pair of adjacent dots.

3. Player #1 always makes a vertical link.

4. Player #2 always makes a horizontal link.

5. No dot can be linked more than once.

6. The first player unable to move loses.

Variations
Try a grid of six × six, seven × seven, or eight × eight.

Battleship (ages 8 and up)
You sunk my battleship! It's the classic game of battleship without having to bring the box full of game pieces. The board game actually began as a pen-and-paper game. All you need to play are four pieces of paper and two pens. Each player has two sheets of paper.

The object is to "hit" your opponent's ships on their grid by making strategic guesses as to where they are.

1. On all four sheets of paper, create grids eleven × eleven, with the top row marked 1 to 10, the side marked A to J. (The left-hand corner square will be blank.)

2. Each player gets the following:
   - 1 carrier (5 squares)
   - 2 battleships (4 squares each)
   - 3 destroyers (2 squares each)
   - 2 cruisers (3 squares each)
   - 1 submarine (3 squares)

3. On one grid, outline all your own ships, not letting the other player see.

4. Take turns trying to guess the other's coordinates.

5. Mark down the guesses on the other grid.

6. When one player hits all the squares of a ship, it's been sunk, and its owner must announce that the ship has been sunk.

7. The first person to sink all the opponent's ships wins.

Aggression *(ages 8 and up)*

This cool game was inspired by the board game Risk and invented by game designer Eric Solomon. Players position armies on a map of countries. They then take turns fighting battles to take control of as many countries as possible. It is helpful to have three different colored pens or pencils for this game.

1. On a sheet of paper, take turns drawing countries to create a map. The countries can have any shape or position, but they must be adjacent to at least one other country. Continue until twenty countries have been created. Label the countries A to T, or give them short names.

2. Each player has one hundred armies and will put some in each country. To do this, each player writes the number of armies in the country you want to occupy. Only one player can occupy each country. Continue claiming countries and allocating your armies until all countries are occupied or both players have allocated all their armies. If you only have one pen and cannot differentiate by color, you can put a circle or square (or triangle) around your number of armies to designate to whom they belong.

3. Now the battle begins. Decide who will begin. Take turns attacking an adjacent country occupied by your opponent. (To count as adjacent, the two countries must have a visible length of common border.) You may conquer a country if you have more armies in your country than in the one under attack. When you attack, cross out the number of armies in the conquered country. Those armies can no longer be used. The number of your attacking armies remains the same. Each turn is one attack.

4. Continue until neither player can make any more conquests. The winner is the player with the largest number of occupied countries.

Paper & Pencil Battle *(ages 10 and up)*

This is an epic war game on paper for older kids. It is helpful to have a ruler or tape measure for this one, but if you don't have one, you can make a measuring stick.

1. Fold a piece of paper in half hamburger style (versus hot dog style—portrait versus landscape). Unfold it and draw a line over the crease.

2. Players draw a fort on their side of the paper (a half box on the edge of the paper with a flag).

3. Players then draw five soldiers on their side. These can be stick figures.

4. The object of the game is to take out the opponent by "shooting" that person's players and fort.

5. During your turn, draw a straight line no longer than 3 inches (your "bullet") on your side of the field that you think will touch your opponent's soldiers or fort when the paper is folded over.

6. Once you have your bullet drawn, fold the paper over.

7. If it touches an opponent's soldier (head or body, *not* legs or arms), that soldier is destroyed.

8. If it hits the opponent's fort, draw an X or a dot to show your hit it. After five hits the fort is destroyed.

9. The opponent then takes her turn.

10. A person wins when all the other player's soldiers and fort are destroyed.

Rules:

- You must make your fort on the EDGE of your side of the paper.
- You cannot fold the paper over before you shoot to check your shot.
- Hits in the limbs don't count.
- Hits on the flag or flagpole don't count.

Connect Four *(ages 6 and up)*

Try a new twist on another classic by playing it on paper.

Make a grid of squares or circles seven across and six down (forty-two total). Use Xs and Os, player initials, or two colors of pen. Play starts at the bottom of the grid. Player #1 marks a space in the bottom row. Player #2 can play on another space in that row or on top of Player #1's space. Play continues in this fashion. The first player to claim four consecutive spaces vertically, horizontally, or diagonally wins.

M.A.S.H. *(ages 8 and up)*

Be a fortuneteller or have your future told right there at your campsite in this paper-and-pencil game. I foresee lots of fun in your future!

1. Player #1 is the "Fortuneteller." She writes "M.A.S.H." (for Mansion, Apartment, Shack, and House) in columns at the top of the paper.

2. Both players contribute to writing a list of categories in a row below the title. Some examples are spouse, number of kids, job, type of car, location, years of employment— really, anything that might indicate the prospective life of the player (movies starred in, income, color of your car). Six categories is a good number, but you can include more.

3. Player #2 thinks of four answers for each category and writes them in a column under the category title. The fortuneteller adds another answer. You can make your options serious or ridiculous.

4. When all the spots are filled, the Fortuneteller begins to draw a spiral either at the bottom of the page or on another piece of paper. After at least 3 seconds, Player #2 chooses a time to say "Stop."

5. The Fortuneteller draws a line through the spiral and counts how many times the spiral intercepts the line drawn. This is the magic number.

6. The Fortuneteller counts each item down the page (starting with the M.A.S.H.) and crosses off the answer she lands on when she gets to the magic number. For instance, if five lines were counted in the swirl, every fifth answer is crossed off the list. This continues until there is only one item in each category. Each letter in the title M.A.S.H. is considered an answer and should be crossed off accordingly.

7. The remaining items are Player #2's future.

8. Now the fortuneteller can read Player #2's fortune. **Example of a fortune:** You will marry **the president**, move to **Disneyland**, and live in a **shack**. You will have **seven**

kids and drive around in a **chartreuse garbage truck.** You will work as a **ditch digger** until the age of **65,** when you'll retire.

9. Switch so that Player #2 becomes the Fortuneteller. Tell other campers' fortunes!

Variations

- **Choose your number.** Instead of a spiral, you can close your eyes and dot the paper until someone tells you to stop and then count how many dots you have. Or do the same with tally marks. Or you can draw a card from a deck of playing cards.

- **Paper Bag Fortune.** You will need a bag or container for each category. Cut out each item in each category and put the slips of paper into a designated bag/container. People getting their fortune told take one slip of paper from each bag and hand the slips to the Fortuneteller without looking at them. The Fortuneteller uses what's on the slips to tell the person's fortune.

24 *(ages 8 and up)*

This game will wake up even a morning brain and can really add up to fun! It can be played by yourself or with multiple players.

1. On pieces of paper about the size of index cards, write down sets of four numbers up to the number 13. Numbers can be repeated. Here are some sample sets of numbers to start with: (1, 2, 3, 4) (4, 5, 6, 2) (6, 1, 2, 2) (3, 8, 3, 2) (2, 10, 2, 1) (8, 7, 5, 4) (10, 15, 4, 2) (1, 9, 9, 12)

2. Put the papers face down on the table.

3. When all players are ready, each takes a piece of paper and flips it over.

4. The object of the game is to use all four numbers on the card and have it come out to 24.

5. You can use addition, subtraction, multiplication, and division, whatever works. Just make sure you use all four numbers, but only once.

6. For example, if you're using (5, 6, 7, 1): $5 \times 6 = 30 - 7 = 23 + 1 = 24$!

7. Whoever gets the answer right first wins the round. (Try noncompetitive play with kids of varying ages.)

8. The winners of the first and second round play against each other next. Keep playing rounds until there is one winner left.

9. If playing solo, try to solve as many as possible in a row, or time yourself and beat your time. Of the 1,820 combinations of numbers, 1,362 (about 75 percent) have solutions.

10. If playing as a group, make sure each combination does make 24 somehow and then switch.

Variation

- Play in pairs.

- Each player secretly writes two numbers between 1 and 13 on a piece of paper.

- Players simultaneously reveal the numbers and try to reach exactly 24 by combining the four numbers using only addition, subtraction, multiplication, and division.

- The first player to announce a solution wins. If neither can come up with a solution, it is a draw.

Function Game *(ages 10 and up)*

One player tries to guess the other player's mathematical rule in this game of numbers and patterns.

1. The Chooser thinks of a rule that converts one number into another (a mathematician would call this a "function").

2. The Guesser then tries to guess the rule by testing it with different numbers. For example, if the Chooser thought of the rule "double it and add one," the game might proceed as follows:

   • Guesser: "1"; Chooser: "3"
   • Guesser: "2"; Chooser: "5"
   • Guesser: "10"; Chooser: "21"
   • Guesser: "100"; Chooser: "201"
   • Guesser: "I think the rule is 'double and add one.'" Chooser: "Correct!"

3. The rule can be anything you like, but sometimes the Guesser may have to guide the Chooser in the right direction; for example: "Try something larger," or "Try a negative number."

Here are some other suggested math rules for the Chooser:

• The number of letters in the word for the number (guess: 6; answer: 3).
• 100 minus the number squared (guess: 9; answer: 19).
• The number reversed (guess: 17; answer: 71).

Panagram *(ages 10 and up)*

Players alternate adding a letter to a word to make an anagram (AN-uh-gram) of a new word. An anagram is a word, phrase, or sentence formed from another by rearranging its letters: *Angel* is an anagram of *glean*.

1. The first player starts with a three-letter word.

2. The next player tries to find a four-letter word by adding a letter and making an anagram of all the letters.

3. The players continue in this way, making longer and longer anagrams. The first player unable to make a word loses.

Example:

• First player starts with: CAT
• The other player adds a K to make: TACK
• Play might continue as follows:
  TRACK
  RACKET
  RACKETS
• Finally the second player makes:
  TRACKERS
• The first player cannot make another word, so the second player wins.

Psst ... Kids! There are 600 common three-letter words, but "fix" and "ivy" can't be extended to four letters, so it's a good idea to ban these as starting words.

Word Square (ages 7 and up)

Create the most word squares from the same set of letters as the other players to win!

1. Players draw a four × four grid (sixteen squares) on a piece of paper, which they keep concealed from the other players.

2. Players take turns naming a letter. As each letter is named, players must write it immediately into one of the squares in their grid. Players can choose any letter they like, and letters can be repeated.

3. When the grid is full, the players count up the number of four-letter words they have made, reading across, down, or diagonally. The player with the highest score (out of a possible 10) wins.

4. Strategy: You can either choose letters that help you complete words or try to thwart your opponent's words.

Word Ladders (ages 9 and up)

A word ladder is a sequence of words in which only one letter changes at each step to make another word. Try to make your ladder the shortest to the top in this fun word game!

1. One player chooses a starting word; the other player then chooses an ending word with the same number of letters.

2. Both players then try to make a word ladder between the two words. Each step consists of a single letter substitution, which must result in another word.

3. The player with the shortest ladder wins.

4. If the ladders are the same length, the game is a tie.

5. If neither player can find a ladder, the game is a draw.

Example:

If the two words are COLD and WARM, one solution to the word ladder puzzle is:

COLD → CORD → CARD → WARD → WARM

Variations

- To make the game more exciting, impose a time limit of 5 minutes.

- For a more complicated variation of the game, try **Scrambled Word Ladders.** Players have the choice of changing one letter to make another word, just as in **Word Ladders,** or scrambling the order of the letters to make another word.

Did You Know?

Word Ladders Origin

Word Ladders were invented by Lewis Carroll, author of *Alice in Wonderland* and *Through the Looking-Glass.* He also called them Doublets. The famous children's author was also a talented mathematician. In his diary he says he invented Doublets on Christmas Day in 1877. He first published his Doublets in *Vanity Fair* magazine and then created a book full of them.

Art Gallery *(ages 4 and up)*

This noncompetitive picture-drawing game is a fun way to bring campers of all ages together. It's also a great icebreaker when settling into camp. No art critics allowed!

1. Each player starts with a blank sheet of paper.
2. The players then take turns in naming an object, which all players must incorporate into their drawing. Players should wait until everyone has finished drawing before naming the next object.
3. The next player names another object to incorporate into the drawing.
4. At some agreed upon point, usually when one player cannot fit any more objects into his picture, all players agree to stop and reveal their drawings.

Consequences *(ages 8 and up)*

This mystery story game can get really wild! The object of the game is to fill in a template story with your own characters, descriptions, and actions.

1. The first player writes down a word or phrase to start a story based on the template that follows or one you make up.
2. Write on the first line and fold the paper over so your word or phrase can't be seen by the other players.
3. Take turns with one or more people to choose a word or phrase to complete the story.
4. Fold over the paper after each word or phrase is written so that nobody knows how the story is shaping up.

The Template

Although there are lots of variations on any story, here's a common pattern to start with:

- Adjective for a person
- Name of a person
- Met (In a standard game, two characters always meet, but you could adjust this to another verb.)
- Adjective for a person
- Name of person
- Where they met
- First person wore
- Second person wore
- First said to second
- Second replied
- The consequence was . . . (a description of what happened after)
- What the world said

When you have added all the parts of the story, unfold the paper and read it aloud.

Monster Makers *(ages 4 and up)*

With each person drawing a different part of its body, who knows what this monster will look like!

1. Take a sheet of paper, hold it portrait style (hot dog style not hamburger), and fold it into thirds.
2. On the top third of the sheet, the first player draws a head. Extend the neck lines just below the fold. The other player(s) should NOT see what has been drawn.
3. When done, that player hands it to the next person, with the middle fold exposed so

that the head is not seen but the neck lines are clear.

4. This next player draws a body, extending the lines for legs just beyond the fold.

5. When done, that player hands it to the next person, with the bottom fold exposed so that neither the head nor body is seen.

6. This player draws legs and feet.

7. All players can add background as well as the figure.

8. When the bottom section is done, unfold the paper and look at your monster creation!

Variation

Monster Flip Book. After several rounds of Monster Makers, stack your papers together and cut along the folds of each sheet from right to left, leaving at least an inch UNCUT on the left. Poke holes into the left margin; thread a grass, reed, or string through each hole; and tie it to hold your book together. Or tape your book together.

Now flip through your book, looking at the top third of one page, the middle of a second, and the bottom of a third, and you have even more crazy combinations of creatures!

Words from a Word *(ages 6 and up)*

Create as many words as you can out of one word. You can do this on your own, compete with others, or play in teams.

1. Players each think of a long word or phrase, write it down on a piece of paper, and put their papers face down on a table or in a container.

2. Each player needs paper and a pen or pencil.

3. If playing as a timed game, you will need a watch or stopwatch. Decide how long everyone has. You might start with 1 minute.

4. One player chooses one of the papers with the words on them and turns it over. Another player starts the timer.

5. Players or teams of players try to make as many words as they can in 1 minute out of the letters of that word or phrase.

6. The player or team that makes the most words wins.

If the word is MONSTER, you could make STORE, ON, ONE, REST, NEST . . .

Rules:

- A letter can only be used as often as it appears in a word. Since MONSTER has only one E, it can be used only once in a word.
- Proper nouns, like names of people or states, don't count.
- Try it untimed.

Chomp *(ages 8 and up)*

This will make you hungry! Take turns chomping into an imaginary bar of chocolate, but watch out for that last bite! It'll get ya!

1. Draw a rectangular grid of squares representing a bar of chocolate, four × three.
2. Mark the top left square with an X. This square is poison!
3. Players take turns taking bites out of the bottom right corner of the bar by marking a square, together with all the squares below and to the right of it.
4. If you have two different-color pens or pencils, shade each square. If you don't, write in your initials.
5. The player forced to eat the poisonous bite loses.

Variation

- Play with a real bar of chocolate!

Classic Games

Though this book primarily encourages do-it-yourself (DIY) games and art inspired by the outdoors, we would be remiss not to mention a few classic card and dice games. It is a longstanding tradition to play card and dice games while camping, and for good reason. They are fun, often challenging, and bring people together.

Psst . . . Kids! Like chess or checkers? Bring along a board and challenge your parents at the picnic table. You can even have a long-running chess game going over several days if activities keep you away from the campsite.

Card Games

When it comes to card games that use a standard fifty-two-card deck, there are many great games for the family. We just don't have room to include the rules for them all in this book,

Photos by Kevin Meynell

but here are a couple of favorites and suggestions for more to look up.

Crazy Eights *(all ages, but especially good for younger campers)*

Crazy Eights is great for families with younger campers, but is fun for kids of all ages. It is a lot like Uno, but only 8s are wild.

1. Dealer passes out seven cards face down to everyone (if there are only two players, each gets five cards instead) then places the deck face down in the center and draws the top card, placing it face up next to the deck. This is the starter card.

2. The player to the dealer's left must play a card from his hand that matches the starter card, either in suit or in denomination. Thus, if the queen of hearts is the starter, any heart or any queen may be played on it. You can only play one card at a time.

3. The next player must play a card that matches the one just played.

4. Eights are wild. Whoever plays an 8 card can decide what suit (hearts, clubs, diamonds, or spades) needs to be played next. The next player must play either a card of the specified suit or another 8.

5. If at any time a player has no card to play (i.e., none that matches in suit or number), the player must draw from the deck until finding a card to play, thus increasing the number of cards in her hand. (When the deck runs out, shuffle all played cards except the top one and place them face down to replenish.)

6. The first player that has no cards left wins the game.

Spoons

This fast-paced card game of matching and sometimes bluffing is played with three or more people and spoons from your camping kitchen.

Supplies: Cards, spoons from your camping kitchen (one fewer than the number of players)

1. In the center of your table, put one fewer spoon than there are players. The dealer passes out four cards to all players and puts the rest of the deck face down within his reach.

2. The dealer draws the top card from the pile and either discards it face down to the player on his left or exchanges it with a card in his hand, in which case he discards that card.

3. The player beside him picks up the discarded card and either exchanges or discards it to the player to her left, and so on. Players try to make their four cards into a set of four of a kind (like four queens or four 2s). Players can only hold four cards plus one from the discard pile at any time.

4. When a player has four of a kind, she can grab a spoon. She might want to try doing it discreetly. When the other players see someone has grabbed a spoon, they can try to grab one too. One person will be without a spoon.

5. If you wish to keep score, players get a letter in the word *spoon* each time they are spoon-less. When they spell the word *spoon* (basically after five losses), they are out.

Variations

- Allow bluffing. Players can reach for spoons but not touch them to try to get other players to grab spoons prematurely. If someone touches a spoon without having four of a kind at the table, she gets a letter in the word *spoon*.

- If playing with a group of six or more, use two decks of cards.

Photos by Kevin Meynell

Number Games. For some fun mathematical challenges, try Chase the Ace, 31 (also known as Scat, Blitz, and Ride the Bus), 99, Hole Golf, Kings in the Corner, and Sequence.

Lasting Classics. More-involved games that will last a lifetime are Gin, Gin Rummy, Cribbage, Hearts, Casino, Black Jack, and Poker—specifically Texas Hold 'Em—Euchre, Whist, and Spades (you can use rocks for chips).

Specialty Cards. The beauty of cards is that they pack light and game play possibilities are vast. Consider some of these specialty decks: Uno, Spot It! (there's even a camping version), Set, Get Bit, Pit, Dutch Blitz, One Up, Citadels, Quiddler, Boggle, Bang!, Sushi Go!, Love Letter, Coup, and Five Crowns.

Card Games for Families with Young Players

Crazy Eights is a lot of fun to play. Some other winners for the younger set are Go Fish, Old Maid, War, Snap, and Concentration (or Memory Game).

Lively Games. Spoons is a camping favorite. Other lively games include I Doubt It (also known as BS and Cheat), Nertz, Slapjack, Speed (also known as Spit or Slam), and Pig.

Dice Games

Taking very little room to pack, regular six-sided dice can yield a bunch of fun games. Most work better if you have paper and a pencil to keep score. You can use camping mugs or cups for shaking and

COOPERATIVE GAMES

Rather than play a competitive game with your family, try a cooperative game. There is an increasingly wide array of cooperative games, in which players have to work together to achieve a common goal rather than win or lose against each other. They are adventurous and super fun.

Some titles include Castle Panic, Forbidden Island, Caves and Claws, Bus Depot Diner, The Secret Door, Hanabi, and The Resistance: Avalon. The classic Dungeons and Dragons is another. Check each game for appropriate age level.

releasing dice if you wish. Most games require either two or five dice, but one camping favorite requires six: Farkle (or its near-cousin, 10,000).

Farkle *(ages 8 and up)*

Each player throws the dice and adds up points to try to reach 10,000, but if you don't have a scoring number in your roll, you Farkle! You'll need paper and a pencil for keeping track of the score.

At the beginning of each turn, the player throws all 6 dice at once from a cup. After each throw, you must select at least one scoring die. You can then pass and bank your points, or risk the points earned this turn and roll the remaining dice.

For example, say you roll a 1, 2, 2, 4, 6, 3. The only score is 1=100. That die stays out. You put the other 5 dice back in the cup and

Farkle Scoring	
Dice value	Points
5s	50
1s	100
1, 1, 1	300
2, 2, 2	200
3, 3, 3	300
4, 4, 4	400
5, 5, 5	500
6, 6, 6	600
Four of a kind	1,000
Five of a kind	2,000
Six of a kind	3,000
A straight of 1–6	1,500
Three pairs	1,500
Four of a kind + a pair	1,500
Two sets of three of a kind	2,500

shake and dispense again. This time you have a 2, 2, 2, 4, 5. Three 2s=200 and 5=50. You might want to stop your turn at 350 points and pass the cup and dice on to the next player. Or, if you are feeling lucky, keep rolling with only one die left.

If the player scores all six dice, he has "hot dice" and may continue his turn with a new throw of all six dice, adding to the score he has already accumulated. There is no limit to the number of "hot dice" a player may roll in one turn.

If none of the dice score in any given throw, the player has "farkled" and all points for that turn are lost. So if you had rolled and gotten 150 points your first roll (taking out 2 dice), but your next is 2, 3, 6, 6, this combination yields no score. You farkle and receive zero for the turn.

At the end of the player's turn, the dice are handed to the next player.

Once a player has achieved 10,000 or more, each other player has one last turn to score enough points to surpass that high score.

Two-Dice Games. Especially great for younger campers and only requiring two dice, try Knock Out, Aces in the Pot, Fifty, and Round the Clock. Shut the Box (also known as Canoga, High Rollers, and other names) is another great one for kids of all ages.

Five-Dice Games. Favorites include Blackjack Dice, Pig, Skunk, Yahztee, Liar's Dice, Hearts Dice, and Drop Dead.

CHAPTER 7

OUTBACK ART & CRAFTS

With a little creativity and imagination, you can make all kinds of arts and crafts using found objects in nature or inspired by nature. By all means, bring along paints and a canvas, pencils, and a drawing pad to capture the artistry of a sweeping view, a cascading waterfall, or a mighty tree. But you can also make works of beauty, intrigue, and playfulness simply from what you find around you or by incorporating a few camping supplies. The act of creation is a powerful one to share with your family,

Great art picks up where nature ends.
—Marc Chagall

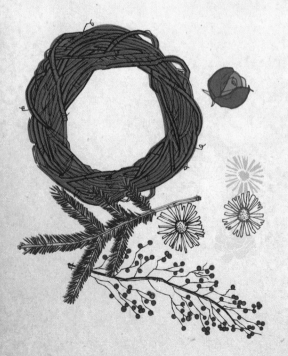

whether you work collaboratively or each express yourselves individually and share your results with one another. So, be a Picasso in the pines! A Monet in the mountains! An O'Keefe out in the open! And have fun expressing yourself naturally.

Be a PHOTOJOURNALIST and take pictures of your art, and have someone take pictures of you creating the art. You can write about them in your NATURE JOURNAL. You can also do any of the art on paper in your Nature Journal. Just remember to give it time to dry before turning the page.

DIY Art Tools Crafted from Nature

Mud Paint
Scoop up dirt or mud with a mini-shovel, plate, pot, or hands. If the dirt is hard, use a stick to pry it up. In a container—extra plastic container, camp cup or bowl, or plastic bag—add water and stir it or knead it with your hands to mix until the mud is the consistency of paint or pancake mix.

Photo by Kevin Meynell

Mud Glue
Make the consistency of your mud paint thicker, more like a paste, and use it to "glue" found and natural objects onto your artwork. Just like glue, remember to give it time to dry!

Making Natural Paints *(ages 3 and up)*
Both science and art, experiment with different plants and organic materials to make watercolors. Young children should be supervised at all times so they do not ingest the paints.

Collect a few kinds of flower petals, herbs, and moss in a variety of colors. Make predictions for each plant: what color it will produce and how bright it will be on paper. Put each one into a ziplock baggie. Heat some water on your camping stove to warm, pour a little (about a quarter of a cup) into each baggie, and seal them, removing excess air. Use a rock or smooth stick to roll and press the plant inside the bag so its color bleeds into the water. You might be surprised. Sometimes the colors that seep out are not the same as the plant itself.

Try out your new paints on paper and see how they look.

Have a little flour or pancake mix in your camping kitchen? Add a little to thicken the brightest paint, and try painting on rocks.

Leaf & Stick Paintbrush
Don't want to get mud or paint on your fingers? Turn leaves and sticks into paintbrushes!

Collect a variety of leaves, sticks, and other woodland debris. Try using each as a brush, or press them to create patterns. Use duct tape to adhere leaves to sticks to create a brush with a handle.

Make It with Mud!

Who needs fancy art supplies when you have . . . MUD! With good old mud, you can make lots of cool art. Whether you like to squish the stuff between your fingers or prefer to stay clean and apply it with a brush made of leaves and sticks or camping utensils, have fun getting creative with mud.

Fork Bear & Friends *(ages 6 and up)*

Use a mud and fork, along with other utensils, to create cute furry creatures and other inhabitants of the forest or ocean!

Supplies:

- Paper
- Mud

- Fork and spoon (butter knife optional)
- Mini pinecones, small rocks, leaves, twigs (optional)

Use a fork as a paintbrush. Dip the bottom of your fork into the mud and run it along the paper from the center outward to make the bear's furry face. Dip the back of a spoon into the mud to make some ears on the top of the bear's head. Create eyes and a nose by either painting them with mud or using mud glue and objects like pebbles, leaves, or acorns. Repurposed paper will work too. Add a bow tie and smile! What else can you make with mud and utensils?

Psst . . . Kids! Make sure you have a way to wash your hands and bowl when you're done.

Lay your drawing out to dry on your picnic table or another flat, dry surface in the sun. Use rocks to weigh down the corners in case of a breeze.

Finger Mud Painting *(ages 2 and up)*

Use mud and your fingers for gooey fun and to make works of art!

Supplies: Paper and mud paint

For this activity, you can try different consistencies of mud. Dip your fingers in the mud and then brush or press them onto a piece of paper. Paint a picture, a pattern, or whatever feels good!

Variation

3-D Mud Painting. Add sticks, leaves, and lichen to your drawing. The heavier the item you are adding, the thicker the mud glue you'll need.

Fingerprint Drawing *(ages 4 and up)*

You can make all kinds of fun critters and characters out of your fingerprints and a few simple lines and shapes with a pen. At the same time, you can check out the cool pattern that is your fingerprint.

The mud for this art project needs to be a bit more watery and less gloppy than for finger painting. Roll your thumb in the mud and press it firmly on a piece of paper. Repeat this as many times as you want. Let the fingerprints dry. Add features to create creatures. With dots for eyes, a wide U for a smile, and squiggly lines for hair, you have a human face. Can you make fish, birds, frogs, rabbits, spiders?

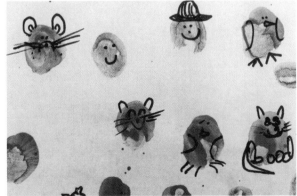

Fingerprint Facts!

No two fingerprints are exactly alike! Most people's fingerprints are patterned in a whorl, loop, or arch. What do your fingerprints look like?

If you can't see them clearly using mud, another great way to examine your fingerprint is to make a heavy mark with a pencil on a piece of paper, roll your finger in it, and then press and slightly roll your finger onto the paper. For an even clearer print, after rolling your finger over the pencil mark, press a piece of scotch tape onto your fingertip, covering part of the sides. Carefully lay the tape onto a sheet of white paper.

Mud Pies *(ages 3 and up)*

It's dirty! It's gooey! It's the art of making mud pies!

Supplies: Dirt, water, a container for making mud, pebbles, flowers and leaves for decoration

Use good smooth dirt fairly free of sand, rocks, and pebbles. Try to make the mud the consistency of bread dough. Knead the mud until it becomes firm enough not to lose shape when you roll it into a small ball. Mold the mud into pies by rolling the mud into balls and flattening down each ball. Decorate your pies with stones, flowers, or leaves.

Mud, Stick, and Leaf Art *(ages 3 and up)*

Can you make a butterfly out of leaves and sticks? How about a camper like you? A fish? A dog? Insects? With your imagination, you can probably make just about anything!

Supplies: Sticks and leaves, paper and mud glue or regular glue

Collect sticks and small branches, leaves, and other woodland debris, and create your work area on a flat surface. Let the objects suggest certain animals or shapes to you. You can even create entire scenes, with people and houses and trees. Set out your sticks and leaves, and make your picture first. Lift each object, apply mud or glue, then press the object back onto the paper.

Variations

- If you don't have paper and glue, you can still make these as temporary art on the picnic table or ground. Be a PHOTOJOURNALIST and take a

picture of your creation before it returns to nature!

- Make your stick and leaf figures in your NATURE JOURNAL. (Keep it open until dry so the pages don't stick.)

- **Make stick and leaf dolls and animals!** You might need a pocketknife to make small cuts into the sticks to hold your leaves, use string to connect them, or use a pinecone as the body. You can even make a log cabin for your leaf dolls.

Art with Rocks

Rocks can suggest all kinds of art projects and provide material for so many crafts. Try some of these as well as some of your own.

Rock Sculptures *(ages 2 and up)*

Got rocks? Be a Michelangelo and make a cool sculpture! This is fun to do along the trail or in camp.

Supplies: Rocks

Pile rocks on top of one another to create rock sculptures. You can start with the largest, flattest rock at the bottom, or you can place large rocks on small ones by finding the balance point. If you do this, it might look as though you are defying gravity.

Variations

- **Game.** See who can create the tallest or most interesting rock sculpture or a rock sculpture that looks like an animal or person.

- Incorporate other found objects, like pinecones and leaves.

- Want a major challenge? Try to create an arch or a bridge.

- Use lots of small rocks or flat rocks to make a **cairn**.

- **Rock Sculpture Garden.** You can leave your sculpture standing and add more throughout your camping trip to create an outdoor sculpture garden.

- **Deconstruction!** When you have finished your sculpture, throw rocks at it and see how many throws it takes to knock it down. Don't destroy other people's sculptures without their permission!

Did You Know?

Rock Balancing as Meditation and More!

Balancing stones is an old Zen technique of examining the mind. Rock balancing can be a performance art, a spectacle, or a devotion, and there are artists who specialize in it.

What Is a Cairn?

A cairn is a man-made pile or stack of stones used as a landmark or memorial, typically on a hilltop or skyline. The word comes from Scottish Gaelic, and the oldest cairns date back to prehistoric times in Eurasia.

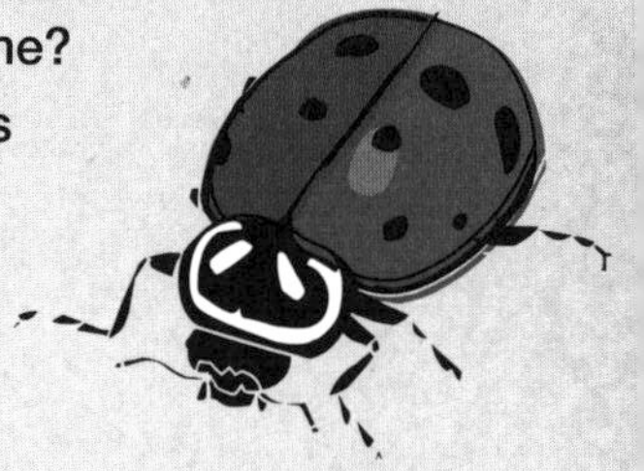

Rock Bugs *(ages 3 and up)*

Some rocks sort of already look like bugs, especially beetles, ladybugs, and spiders. You can finish the job and create cool crawly critters out of rocks!

Supplies:

- Rocks
- Mud or indelible markers
- Sticks for legs and antennae (optional)
- Leaves for wings (optional)
- Glue or mud glue (optional)

Find your rocks. Clean them, wipe them off, and dry them completely. Draw on features with mud on a stick or your finger. If you want, use mud glue and sticks to make legs and leaves on the back for wings.

Variations

- Use natural paints that you make yourself (see page 166).
- Use chalk to draw on the rocks for temporary art.
- Use acrylic paint and base for a more permanent effect and bring your art home.
- **Clay Rocks.** Brought clay or Play-Doh from home? Shape it around rocks to make just about anything. You can also use dots of clay to adhere antennae and legs.

Did You Know?

Painted rock art or pictographs (PIK-tuh-grafs) are one of the oldest known forms of art, dating back to at least 50,000 years ago. The rock art of ancient Sumerian, Egyptian, and Chinese civilizations developed into some of the first written languages, which used pictures to tell stories.

Rock Words *(ages 6 and up)*

Make meaningful gifts for your fellow campers out of rocks and thoughtfully chosen words! Rock Words are simple and powerful.

Supplies:

- Rocks

- Indelible pens (or other markers)
- Chalk or paint (optional)

1. Find rocks you really like. They need to have a surface on which you can write. You might choose rocks that feel good when you hold them in your hand or rocks you like to look at. Wash or wipe off the dirt, and dry them completely. If you have paint, you can paint the rock and let it dry before adding your word, but this is not necessary.

2. Think of a word, a positive adjective, a noun, a verb, or a phrase that describes the person you are making the rock for. **Examples:** LOVING, PLAYFUL, SMART, AMAZING. Think about how long your word is before you start writing to make sure it will fit on the rock. You might even want to write it on a piece of paper first. Write the word with a pen or marker on the rock. Chalk will work too for temporary art. If you wish, decorate with borders, dots, squiggles, stripes, or other decorations. Present it to your friend or loved one!

Variations

- If you used indelible marker, add a nice shine. Ask your parents if you can use a little cooking oil. Place a dab of oil on a paper towel and rub it over the top of your rock.

- Make a rock with each person's name as a table setting.

- Use rocks as camp organizers or reminders. Put ART on one to hold down paper art so it won't blow away. Other rocks could say WASH HANDS, GAMES, NAPKINS, TP, SHOES HERE, and more.

- Have your family make rocks for one another. You could draw names from a hat or have everyone make one for each family member and present them. Make sure all the words are positive descriptions!

Art with Leaves

Leaves come in so many shapes and have beautiful intricate patterns that you can use to create some wonderful arts and crafts.

Leaf Rubbing *(ages 6 and up)*

Make the patterns of leaves come alive in your own artwork!

1. Collect leaves.

2. Arrange one leaf or several leaves on top of a piece of paper taped to the table.

3. Place another piece of paper over your leaves. Hold it in place by taping the corners down, or hold it down securely with your hands.

4. Rub crayons or pencils across it, and watch the pattern of the leaves appear on the paper.

Variations

- Hold a piece of paper up to a rock or side of a tree, and rub to capture those textures.
- Make a collage of several items. You can display these in Natural Frames (page 177).
- Don't have crayons? You can use the black end of a completely cooled piece of burnt wood, natural charcoal.
- Add drawings, doodles, or painted color to your art.

Leaf Silhouettes *(ages 6 and up)*

Tape leaves down on a piece of paper in any way you wish. Paint over and around them with either natural paint, mud paint, charcoal, or paint from home. Let it dry. Carefully remove the leaves to reveal a beautiful silhouette of your leaves.

Variation

Leaf Paintings. Leave the leaves on your paper, securing them with mud or glue, and draw or paint around them to create a mixed-medium work of art.

Leaf Animals

Collect leaves that suggest animals to you: a leaf for the body, for the head, for ears and legs, and other features. Use mud or glue to paste down leaves to a sheet of paper. Add other woodland debris as needed to complete your animal. Or complete by drawing legs and other features around and on the leaves.

Leaf Crown

Make a crown out of paper and duct tape. Use glue or adhere duct tape, sticky side up, all around the crown. Place leaves on the crown to your liking, and be the king or queen of the forest.

Leaf Mobile *(ages 6 and up, although any age can find the leaves)*

Make falling leaves so they never hit the ground with this lovely "moving" work of art.

Supplies:

- Stick about 12 inches long, ¼ inch in diameter (It doesn't have to be straight.)
- Thread, fishing line, or string
- Leaves with stems
- Scissors or blade

1. Find the center point of the stick by testing it to see where it balances on your finger.
2. Tie a string around the center to hang your mobile from when you're done.
3. Wrap a thread around a stem of a leaf several times and knot it to secure.
4. Tie the other end of the thread to somewhere on the stick, hanging to the desired length.

5. Continue adding leaves until the stick is balanced and you like the look.

Variation

Leaf Garland. This is a little simpler to make. Cut a string to the size garland you want. Cut small lengths of thread; tie one end to a stem of a leaf and the other end to a place on the string. Keep adding leaves until you like the look of your garland and then hang it up.

Art with Sticks

Sticks come in so many shapes and sizes that you can create just about anything with them!

Magic Wand *(ages 3 and up)*

Woods are enchanting places full of intrigue and magic. Make your own wand to cast spells and make the magic appear.

Supplies:

- A special stick
- A pocketknife or potato peeler (optional)
- Felt-tip pens, Sharpies, or mud (optional)
- Any of the following: duct tape, rope, string, ribbon, leaves, feathers, pine needles

Search for a stick that feels like it could become a wand, one that feels good in your hand. If you wish, peel the bark off the stick. Sometimes you can do this with your fingers. If not, you or a parent can use a pocketknife or other sharp tool to peel off all the bark or peel it off in places to make rings of bark. Older kids can use a pocketknife to carve magic words, symbols, or patterns into their wands. Use a Sharpie or felt-tip pen to write and draw on and color your wand. You can wrap duct tape or string around your wand for decoration or to create a grip. Tie ribbons, scrap material, paper, yarn, feathers, leaves, special rocks, or whatever you wish onto your wand to decorate it. You can dangle items from it as well. Now, give it a swish!

Journey Stick *(ages 3 and up)*

When Australian Aboriginals would go on long journeys, they tied objects to a stick. Starting at one end of the stick and working along it as they traveled, they would create a story timeline. The objects helped them remember events and experiences on their journey so they could tell others of their adventures.

You can also wrap duct tape around part of your stick with the sticky side out, securing it at top and bottom with tape sticky side down. Just press on leaves, twigs, small rocks, or other small objects of significance. This makes it easy for young explorers.

Around the campfire or back home, have the family gather round as you tell the story of your adventure using your journey stick.

Stick Creatures *(ages 3 and up)*

Add eyes, mouth, and other details using paints (or pens) to bring a stick to life.

Supplies:

- Sticks
- Indelible markers or acrylic paints (or other paints or pens)
- Brushes
- String or yarn (optional)

1. Collect sticks in different shapes. (Driftwood is great because it is already without bark.)
2. Strip any bark, and wipe down the wood to remove dirt.
3. Paint a base coat of one color and allow it to dry.
4. Over this color, paint or draw on eyes, mouth, and any other details you want (hair, nose, clothes, jewelry, random patterns like stripes and polka dots).
5. Let your creatures dry and use them to decorate your campsite.
6. Don't have paint? Just make a stick creature a bit more au natural. Strip the bark and use markers or mud to decorate.

People in many other countries create journey sticks too. Now it's your turn to create your own journey stick for a hike or to tell the story of your camping experience!

Supplies:

- Sturdy stick
- Duct tape and/or string or yarn
- Markers, paint, indelible pens, pocketknife (optional)

Use string to tie objects to the stick that help you remember what you saw and did. You can add different colors with yarns or paint or pens to represent not only different experiences but also your feelings about them.

7. Enjoy your creatures at home, or leave them in interesting places for other people to discover.

Variations

- Wrap yarn or string around the stick for clothing, or attach it for hair.
- Leave the bark on in places for clothes or other features.
- They don't have to be creatures. You can just make beautiful colored and decorated sticks.
- You can do the same with rocks or leaves.
- Have an extra deck of cards? Use indelible markers or acrylic paint to alter the faces of the face cards. Add tails and legs, snouts, and beaks to turn them into animals.

Natural Frames

Create a beautiful frame for your campground artwork or a photograph of your camping trip using sticks and other woodland treasures! Use your imagination and the resources around.

Stick Frame. Find four sturdy, interesting-looking sticks that are slightly longer than each side of your artwork. Lay them out to figure out which sticks go in front and back in the way you like best. The sticks should overlap at the corners. Make sure the back two parallel sticks lie somewhat flat. Wrap string to tie them at the corners, or secure with tape (weave the corners like a God's eye—see page 179—for another look). String on or glue on decorations if you wish.

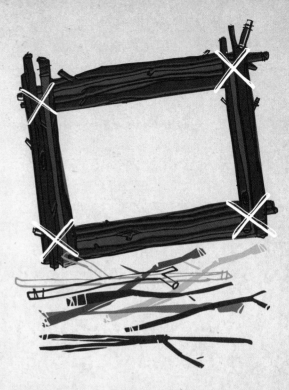

Variations

- **Painted Stick Frame.** Whittle the chosen sticks before starting your frame, and paint them or color them with indelible markers. Secure with strings, duct tape, or glue.
- **Log Cabin or Raft Frame.** String together several sticks on each side. You can tie small pinecones, feathers, acorns, leaves or needles (that will dry well), or small rocks as decoration anywhere you want on the frame. Secure them by running the strings between the sticks and securing to the back of the frame.
- **Duct Tape Frame.** There's SO much you can make from this handy camping supply item! You will be attaching duct tape sticky side up to sticky side down to create the sides of the frame, attaching it at the corners with more duct tape. An option

is to attach another layer of tape sticky side up to the front and stick on woodland debris, even small pinecones, to decorate.

- **Rock Frame.** Find a large rock that is flat or mostly flat on one side. Pour some glue in a container, and add water to thin it into a brushable liquid. (If using mud glue, just adhere the art by its edges or corners so it doesn't get too saturated.) Place your artwork on the rock until you like how it looks. Turn your artwork over, and brush on a light coat of the glue mix. Turn it over and adhere it to the rock, pressing and smoothing it out. If you used indelible ink, you can gently brush the glue mix over your artwork until it is covered completely to give it a shiny look.

Art with Pinecones

Pinecones are so pretty as is, you can use them to make a centerpiece for the table. Here are some other ideas for pinecone crafts.

Pinecone Ornaments

Even at its simplest, a pinecone on a string can be lovely. But you can also decorate pinecones in countless ways. Hang them around camp, or bring them home to give as gifts or souvenirs!

Ideas for decorating your pinecone ornament:

- Tuck leaves, small colorful rocks, twigs, or feathers in the pinecone. Use glue or mud to keep them in place.
- Stick two or three leaves in the top, adhering them with glue, to give your pinecone an apple look.
- Use twigs, leaves, and small rocks or acorns to create faces and limbs.
- Stick a bunch of twigs out from your pinecone to make it a prickly star.
- Color and cut out shapes in paper to decorate your pinecone with random

designs or to make them look like various animals.

- Use string to create a pinecone garland.
- When you get home, paint a pinecone and add glitter, sequins, or ribbon to decorate.
- Make a pinecone mobile.
- What else can you think of?

Pinecone Photo and Nametag Holders

Use pinecones as lovely natural holders to display your art and photos. The holder itself may inspire the art!

Supplies:

- Pinecones
- A base (rock, bark, driftwood, pine needles, leaves, small rocks)
- Your art
- Cardboard or duct tape
- Glue (optional)

After completing your artwork in camp, glue cardboard to the back or adhere duct tape to the back to make it stiff. Find an open pinecone that will hold your work of art. Collect small stones or needles to pile around your pinecone to keep it upright.

Variation

Use open pinecones to create nametags and word art at the table in the same way.

Art with String

These beautiful art projects require string, yarn, or fishing line. The weaving can be very relaxing and pleasurable. And each creation will be unique, like you!

God's Eyes *(ages 5 and up)*

The Pueblo and other Native Americans wore this special decoration that they called a God's eye (*ojo de Dios*). It was thought to be a magical item, bringing good luck and long life. You can make these fun and colorful creations out of string and sticks!

Supplies: String, 2 sticks of similar length

1. Place two sticks together to form an X. This is the frame for the God's eye.
2. Tie one end of the yarn around the center of the frame to hold them together. Make the knot tight so the sticks aren't loose.
3. Hold the frame in one hand and keep the sticks in place.
4. With the other hand, wrap the yarn over and around one arm of the X, then over and around the next arm, and so on. Pull the yarn tightly each time, and push the yarn down snugly toward the center.
5. Continue working this way until the God's eye is completed.

6. Change colors by knotting a new color yarn to the old one. Or use a multicolor yarn.

7. Cut the yarn 3 inches from the end of the God's eye. Use your fingers or a quilter's needle to tuck the end into the back of the God's eye to secure.

8. Leave as is, or finish the ends with pom-poms, tassels, or bows, tied or glued on.

Did You Know?

Awesome Facts about Ojos de Dios (God's Eyes)

During Spanish colonial times in New Mexico, from the 1500s to the 1800s, *ojos de Dios* were placed where people worked and where they walked along a trail. In many of the pueblos of New Mexico today *ojos de Dios* are still created for celebrations, gifts, or blessings for a home.

In Mexico, the Huichol Indians weave God's eyes and call them *tzicuri* or *sikuli*, which means "the power to see and understand things unknown." They make them primarily to heal and protect children. The four points represent natural elements: earth, fire, air, and water. The colors have different meanings too: red = life itself; yellow = sun, moon, and stars; blue = sky and water; brown = soil; green = plants; black = death.

Variation

Branch Weaving. Use a forked stick and weave the yarn from one side to the other, wrapping the yarn around each branch to secure it. Try weaving in different patterns too.

Dream Catcher *(ages 9 and up)*

It is said that a dream catcher protects a sleeping person from negative dreams while letting positive dreams through. The positive dreams slip through the hole in the center of the dream catcher and glide down the feathers to the sleeping person below. The negative dreams get caught up in the web and vanish when the first rays of the sun strike them.

You can make a dream catcher out of sticks or a paper plate.

Supplies: Sticks; string or yarn; beads, feathers, acorns, ribbons to decorate

1. Use string to tie some pliable sticks, overlapping them and wrapping string around where they overlap and knotting it. Do this until you make a hoop.

2. Measure out seven points equidistance on the hoop.

3. Tie a string to one of the points and wrap it around to secure it.

4. Skip two points and wrap the string and knot it at the third point, making sure it is taut, but doesn't pull on the hoop.

5. Keep doing this until you have reached all the points.

6. If you have a bead (or make one by poking a hole in an acorn shell), string it on between points to represent a spider.

7. Add ornaments of feathers, acorns, or rocks hung by strings to the bottom of the hoop.

8. Use another string to tie at the top to hang it by.

Variation

Paper Plate Dream Catcher. This is easier for younger campers. Use eleven points. Cut out the center to leave a ring or hoop. Have the artist decorate the ring with crayons or pens before you start stringing it.

Finger Knitting *(ages 5 and up)*

With a little string or yarn, you can make a beautiful, thick woven rope that could be a belt, scarf, keychain, and more. This is a great solo activity. If you enjoy this, look for more-advanced types of finger weaving online.

1. Wrap the end of your yarn around your index finger twice.

2. Take the bottom loop over the top loop, but not over your finger.

3. Take what is now the bottom loop over the top loop and the top of your finger, and slide it down to make a slipknot.

4. Pull the tail between your fingers to the back of your hand out of the way.

5. Wrap the yarn all the way around your middle finger, ring finger, and pinkie finger.

6. Go back the opposite way, wrapping each finger again, so each finger has two strands on them except the pinkie.

7. Bend your index finger, and pull the bottom loop over the top one and the finger. Do this on the other two fingers.

8. Next wrap the yarn around the middle finger, ring finger, and pinkie finger so each has two strands (and the index finger doesn't). Pull the bottom loops over the tops ones on each finger again.

9. Repeat this until you have the number of rows you want.

10. To finish it off, cut the string about 12 inches from your hand. Put the end through each loop and pull it off the finger. Cinch it up. Put the end of the yarn through the last weave, leaving a loop. Put the end through the loop to knot it.

Wind Chimes *(ages 6 and up)*

Use sticks, rocks, found objects, repurposed trash, or extras from the camping kitchen to make a wind chime.

Supplies:

- Sticks, pinecones, rocks, found objects, repurposed trash, camping kitchen extras
- String

Find a sturdy stick to hang your chimes from. Look for natural objects first. You will have to experiment to find sticks that have some resonance and sound good when they hit each other, perhaps because they are a little hollow. Try gently knocking together these natural objects.

Try other objects: extras from the camping kitchen, found pieces of glass (not sharp), shells, old tin cans, nails, jar lids, shells, beads, silverware, bells, etc.

Tie objects so they dangle a few inches from the base stick. Tie another string from the base stick to hang it up from. You will have to find the balance point. Hang them up in the wind and listen to the beautiful music you've created, or just enjoy the movement in the breeze.

Variation

Use a similar technique to make a mobile.

Word Garland *(ages 6 and up)*

Create a Word Garland to decorate your campsite or remind everyone of a special value.

Cut pieces of paper about 4 inches by 2 inches (or any size you want). Fold them in half and decorate both sides with color or add decorative borders. Drape them over a piece

Did You Know?

Similar garlands known as Tibetan prayer flags can be found in any country where the Buddhist religion is practiced, especially along mountain ridges and peaks high in the Himalayas. They date back to Bon, an ancient religion in Tibet before Buddhism. Often made from colorful rectangular pieces of cloth, traditional prayer flags include woodblock-printed text and images. They are used to promote peace, compassion, strength, and wisdom.

of string. Write a letter on each piece of paper to create a significant word or phrase. It could be someone's name, a word like LOVE, or a funny or meaningful saying. Glue inside the fold so some glue is on the string too, and place your papers where you want them on the string. Put your garland up somewhere in camp for all to see!

Jewelry

Make accessories for yourself or a member of your family out of natural objects. They can be beautiful and a reminder of your camping trip and the beautiful scenery you saw. With help from parents when needed, these can be made by campers of any age. Though you'll find only a couple examples here, you can probably come up with all kinds of jewelry if you have string, nature, and your imagination!

Rock Necklace

Make a beautiful and simple necklace out of a rock or shell and some string. It's cool enough to wear post-camp!

Supplies:

- String or twine
- A special rock or seashell
- Glue (optional)

1. Cut a piece of string about 1 yard in length. If it is thin string, you might want to braid it first for strength and a cool look.
2. Find a rock or seashell you like.
3. Glue the center of the string to the back of the rock, and wrap the string around the rock multiple times, making a pattern you like and securing the rock.
4. As you wrap, make sure to keep the two ends of string even.
5. Tie the two ends together in a small knot to secure the rock. If necessary, cut the string to a comfortable length for your necklace and tie it in the back.
6. Let the glue dry before wearing.

Variation

You can also wrap your rock or shell with a separate string and string it onto your necklace. Using this method, you can dangle more than one object if you wish.

Nature Charm Bracelet

Make a string bracelet, braiding it or triple-wrapping it comfortably around your wrist. With other pieces of string, tie found objects onto your bracelet to create a nature charm bracelet. You can make necklaces and rings the same way!

Musical Instruments

You can find musical instruments ready to use in your camping kitchen or discover them as found objects in the landscape around you. You can make them out of repurposed camping supplies and natural items. They are just what you need to make a little rhythm or form a campground band.

Found Instruments

Got pots and pans? Sticks? Plastic containers or bags you can fill with rocks? Cups? Spoons? Leaves or blades of grass? All these different things and more can be used as instruments for your campground band.

- **Sticks and rocks.** Hit them together, or use them as drumsticks on a hollow log, large stone, the picnic table, or pots and pans. Hit rocks together. See what different sounds you can make.
- **Pebbles and a cup.** Put a bunch of pebbles in a cup, cover it with your hand, and shake it to make a maraca. Cover the top of a paper cup with duct tape to make it more permanent, and decorate. Attach the cup with duct tape to a short stick to give it a handle.
- **Pots and pans.** Drum on them with a wooden spoon. Try a metal or plastic spoon or a stick and see what different sounds you can get. Try hitting different parts of the pot.

ideal leaf will have a smooth, slightly waxy surface. It should be firm while remaining flexible enough to bend. (Check the type of leaf out with your parents to make sure it is safe.)

2. Stretch the top edge of the leaf tightly across your mouth. Purse your lips in a natural position for blowing air. Don't pucker (like a kiss). Rest the leaf on your bottom lip, bending it slightly to match the contour of your lip.

3. Blow firmly upon the leaf. With your lips pursed, the controlled stream of air should create a high-pitched noise akin to a violin. If no sound is created, make adjustments. Try blowing softer and harder, as well as changing the angle of the leaf and position and shape of your upper and lower lips. The leaf needs to be able to vibrate to make the sound. Once a sound is achieved, maintain this note.

4. Alter the amount of airflow from your mouth to change the note you are playing on the leaf. This is how all notes on a leaf are created. It takes a great amount of practice and breath control to be able to play music accurately on a leaf. Once you can play a few notes, try a melody such as "Row, Row, Row Your Boat" or "Mary Had a Little Lamb."

- **Empty bottles and water.** If you have empty bottles, glass or plastic, try hitting against them with a spoon or stick. Add different amounts of water, and drum them again to change the tones. You can also blow across the tops of empty bottles, like you're playing a flute.

- **Empty plastic milk or water jug and water.** Hit the empty container with a stick or wooden spoon. Now add some water, about a third full or so. Secure the twist-on lid. Put the jug under your arm and drum on it while squeezing it to make the sound change.

Leaf Instrument

Believe it or not, with the right leaf and the right mouth method, you can play entire melodies! In China there are symphonies written that feature a leaf soloist.

1. Find a leaf that is large enough to be held in both hands and pressed to your lips. An

Back at home, look online to see leaf musicians in action.

Variation

You can also make a high-pitched whistle with a **blade of grass**. One method is to hold it firmly between your thumbs and blow at the edge of the grass in the space between.

Generally easier than leaf-blowing, it may only produce one loud note.

Stringed Instrument

Find a sturdy bent or curved stick. Tie string securely to each end, keeping it taut (use one of the knots you learned on page 105). Duct tape can help secure it; a parent might need to make a cut in the end with a pocketknife. If taut enough, the string will vibrate when plucked. The vibration creates the sound. The tighter the string is pulled, the higher the sound. You can also pull a string over the top of a pot or cup or anything hollow. If you have room, add more strings of different tightness on top of the hole to create multiple notes.

Paper Plate Tambourine *(ages 3 and up)*

Shake to the rhythm with your hand-made tambourine.

Supplies:

- 2 paper plates
- Pebbles, seeds

- Duct tape
- Pens, paints (optional)

Gather pebbles or seeds and put a handful or two on top of a paper plate. Put another paper plate on top of the other. Use duct tape to close the edges. Decorate your tambourine. Shake it up and make some rhythm!

Play the Spoons

You need two metal spoons.

1. Hold one of them between your thumb and first finger, with the end of the utensil's handle on your palm and its approximate center crossing over your middle knuckle.

2. Now put the other spoon between your first and middle fingers. Hold this second spoon upside down, so that the bottoms of both spoons can hit each other. (If you have little hands—or big spoons—you might have to put a pair of fingers between the two implements.)

3. Next make a fist and grip the handles of both spoons tightly. Be sure to leave about half an inch between the two spoons' bowls. That way, the convex sides will click together whenever you bang them against a surface, while your tight palm grip will act as a spring to pull the cups apart again afterward.

4. Try striking your leg with the spoons. Did you hear a clicking noise? Put your free hand above the spoons and hit your hand. Go back and forth, hitting your gripped spoons against leg and hand.

5. Start slow and then try a faster rhythm. Keep practicing. To get some different sounds out of your spoons, try hitting them

against other parts of your body, like your belly. Try different patterns.

If you like playing the spoons, go online at home to learn how to get even more sounds out of this instrument.

Straw Flute

1. Flatten the end of a straw between your thumb and finger (about the last inch).

2. Cut the flattened part into a point.

3. Cut off one of the points while leaving the other.

4. Cut some holes along one side of the length of the straw.

5. Play it just like a normal flute: Hold the pointed end in your mouth and place one finger on each hole. Release the fingers from the holes to get different tones.

Variation

Stick Flute. The key is finding the right stick. Look around for a stick 6 to 12 inches long that has soft pith or is hollow in the center. Gouge out the pith (the insides) with a long, slimmer stick. Using a pocketknife or screwdriver (with adult supervision), drill out four holes, about a thumb width apart. Play the flute as though you were blowing into a bottle, or blow across the open end at an angle.

Handmade Kazoo

Take the melody, and make some music with a kazoo.

Comb Kazoo. Get out your comb. Cut a piece of wax paper or plastic bag so it is slightly smaller than the length of the comb and twice the size of the comb's height. Fold the wax

paper in half so it covers the teeth of the comb on both sides of the comb. Secure the paper on the comb with a little tape on the holding end if you wish, but not too tight or you will lose the vibration. Place dry lips against the wax paper and hum and go "dooo" to produce sound. Experiment a little. Adjust the tension of the paper as needed.

Straw Kazoo. Bite on the end of a straight drinking straw in order to flatten it. Cut an upside-down V into the flattened end of the straw. Place the straw into your mouth so that the pointed end of the V is securely inside your lips. Blow into the pointed end of the straw gently so that it vibrates and makes a sound like a kazoo.

Toilet Paper Tube Kazoo. Use a pencil to poke a hole in the side of a toilet paper tube, equal distance from either end. (You can also make a tube with cardstock-thick paper and tape.) Cover one end of the tube with a square of plastic grocery bag, and hold it in place with a rubber band. The membrane material should be snug, but not stretched too tightly. Put your lips to the open end and hum or sing. Experiment with different sounds, and adjust the tightness of the membrane if needed.

Family Conversation Starters

- Would you rather stay up late or get up early?
- Would you rather jump into a pool of chocolate pudding or a pool of chocolate ice cream?
- What does it mean to be inspired?
- What is the most beautiful place you've ever seen?
- If you had to write a book, what would you write it about?
- Is there something that you do differently in your family that you are really proud of?
- If you could create a new tradition for our family, what would it be? Or how would you change a family tradition we already have?
- Come up with three silly new traditions for the world. Or for aliens on another planet!

CHAPTER 8

SONGS OF THE WILD

Whether on the trail, on the beach, doing dishes in camp, or sitting around the campfire at night, music can truly enhance your family experience. It is, after all, the "universal language." It can spark great joy and help us express ourselves. It can help make the time go by faster. It can add a bounce to a child's step on the trail. You don't need instruments to sing campfire songs. If no one in your family can sing, try some chanting or repeat-after-me songs.

Besides the classic camping songs included here, make sure to add your pop, rock 'n' roll, and country favorites; songs from your favorite musical; or any genre of music, new or old! This will help to engage your older kids especially. Invite your teenagers to teach you or familiarize you with one of their favorite songs. And then share one of yours. It's a great way to share with one another.

> The earth has music for those who listen.
>
> —George Santayana, poet, novelist, and philosopher

Songs about Camping

Campers of all ages can enjoy these songs, sung to familiar, traditional tunes, but younger campers especially love them. Introduce these songs to your little campers at home before you go to increase enthusiasm about their upcoming adventure.

A-Camping We Will Go

(Sung to "Farmer in the Dell")
You can replace "We" with the name of one of the family members and add different names each verse.

A camping we will go.
A camping we will go.
Hi Ho the Derry-O.
A camping we will go.

We'll pitch the tent right here.
We'll pitch the tent right here.
Hi Ho the Derry-O.
We'll pitch the tent right here.

The second one said, "Let's all go for a cool
   swim."
The third one said, "I'll ask a grown-up to watch
   while we're in."
The fourth one said, "Let's get our safety vests."
The fifth one said, "We're the best."
"O-O-O-O-K," went the parents.
"Yeah," went the kids.
And the five little campers began to swim.

Over the River
(Sung to "Over the River")

Over the river, along the trail,
The hikers march along.
And as they go, they love to sing
Their favorite hiking song.

Over the river, along the trail,
They love to hike and sing.
They're filled with all the wonders
A nature hike can bring.

We'll stack the wood right here.
We'll stack the wood right here.
Hi Ho the Derry-O.
We'll stack the wood right here.

We'll try not to wake the bear. [soft voice]
We'll try not to wake the bear. [softer voice]
Hi Ho the Derry-O. [softer voice]
We'll try not to wake the bear. [softer voice]

Five Little Campers
(Sung to "Five Little Monkeys")
A spoken song—add movements to go with
the words! For example, hold up your fingers
for the number of campers, make a sun with
your arms, give a double thumbs-up for having fun, mock swimming, etc.

Five little campers sitting in the sun,
The first one said, "I'd like to have some fun."

Did You Ever Go A-Camping?

(Sung to "Did You Ever See a Lassie?")
Make up verses of your own.

Did you ever go a-camping, a-camping,
*   a-camping?*
Did you ever go a-camping and sleep in a
*   tent?*
2. . . . and see a raccoon?
3. . . . and hike in the woods?
4. . . . and fish in a boat?
5. . . . and have a campfire?

Campfire Pokey

(Sung to "Hokey Pokey")
You can sing this one while making s'mores!

You put your marshmallow in.
You take your marshmallow out.
You put your marshmallow in and you shake
*   it all about.*
You do the campfire pokey, and you turn your-
*   self about.*
And that's what it's all about, yum, yum!

Replace *marshmallow* with *hot dog, potato,*
apple, popcorn, or anything else you can roast
over a campfire.

Photo by Kevin Meynell

Repeat-after-Me Songs

Whenever you sing or chant this type
of song, the leader starts with "This is a
repeat-after-me song," and all the other
singers say after her: "This is a repeat-
after-me song." Then you're ready to
begin. Take turns with members of your
family as the leader. Many of these repeat-
after-me songs are great accompanied
with movements. Make some up for everyone to repeat along with the words.

By the Campfire

We sat around the campfire (we sat around the
*   campfire)*
On a chilly night (on a chilly night)
Telling spooky stories

In the pale moonlight
Then we added some more logs
To make the fire bright
And sang some favorite camp songs
Together with all our might.
And when the fire flickered and embers began to
   form
We snuggled in our sleeping bags
All cozy, tired, and warm.

Boom Chick a Boom

I said a boom chick a boom.
I said a boom chick a boom.
I said a boom chick-a-rocka chick-a-rocka chick
   a boom.
Oh, yeah
Uh-huh
One more time.
A little louder [or a little lower, higher, faster
   slower, quieter, baby style, with a dialect, you
   decide!] (Repeat)

Bazooka Bubble Gum

My momma
She gave me a dollar
She told me to buy a collar
But I didn't buy no collar.

[All together on this next part. Add some funny
dances!]
Instead - I - bought - some
Bubblegum BAZOOKA, ZOOKA
Bubblegum BAZOOKA, ZOOKA
Bubblegum BAZOOKA, ZOOKA gum!

My momma
She gave me a quarter
She told me to tip the porter
But I didn't tip no porter

Instead - I - bought - some
Bubblegum BAZOOKA, ZOOKA
Bubblegum BAZOOKA, ZOOKA
Bubblegum BAZOOKA, ZOOKA gum!

My momma
She gave me a dime
She told me to buy a lime
But I didn't buy no lime
Instead - I - bought - some
Bubblegum BAZOOKA, ZOOKA
Bubblegum BAZOOKA, ZOOKA
Bubblegum BAZOOKA, ZOOKA gum!

My momma
She gave me a nickel
She told me to buy a pickle
But I didn't buy no pickle
Instead - I - bought - some
Bubblegum BAZOOKA, ZOOKA
Bubblegum BAZOOKA, ZOOKA
Bubblegum BAZOOKA, ZOOKA gum!

My momma
She gave me a penny
She told me to buy some bubblegum
But I didn't buy no bubblegum
Because - I'm- sick - of
Bubblegum BAZOOKA, ZOOKA
Bubblegum BAZOOKA, ZOOKA
Bubblegum BAZOOKA, ZOOKA gum!

Down by the Bay

Down by the bay
Where the watermelons grow
I dare not go
For if I do
My mother will say,

"*Did you ever see a llama wearing pink pajamas?*"
Down by the bay.

Other endings:
Did you ever see a bug drinking from a mug?
Did you ever see a bear wearing underwear?
Did you ever see a fly wearing a tie?
Did you ever see a flower taking a shower?
Did you ever see a moose shaking it loose?
Did you ever have a time when you couldn't make up a rhyme?

Photo by Kevin Meynell

Make up some verses of your own!

Going Fishing

This song might get little campers into the spirit of fishing. As the leader says each line, she can make up movements of the fish, worm, and fisherman. When repeating the line, campers imitate the movements.

When I go fishing down at the brook,
I put a wiggly worm on my hook.

I toss it in the water
And hope with all my might,
A little fish will swim on by
And take a great big bite.

Morning Bird Song

Wake up by singing or chanting this repeat-after-me song with the family while making breakfast. Add movements to stretch!

Way up in the sky the little birds fly
While down in the nest, the little birds rest
With a wing on the left
And a wing on the right
The little birds sleep . . . all through the night.
Shhhhhhhh, they're sleeping.

Then UP comes the sun
The dew falls away
Good morning, good morning, the little birds say.

She says, "Ooh Ahh, Gooshy Gooshy Goo."
She says, "Ooh Ahh, Gooshy Gooshy Goo."
  [accompanied by hip gesticulations]

Down in the jungle where nobody goes
There lives a wishy washy woman washing her
  clothes.
She says, "Ooh Ahh, Gooshy Gooshy Goo."
She says, "Ooh Ahh, Gooshy Gooshy Goo."

Down in the jungle where nobody goes
There lives a wishy washy woman washing her
  clothes.

Washer Woman

A repeat-after-me song sure to bring giggles.
(Everyone dances on the "Gooshy-Gooshy Goo"
parts.)

Down in the jungle where nobody goes
There lives a wishy washy woman washing her
  clothes.

Parody Songs

A parody takes an existing song and
makes it humorous. You can take any song
you know and rewrite it to make it a parody. Give it a try!

On Top of Spaghetti

(Sung to "On Top of Old Smoky")

> *On top of spaghetti,*
> *All covered with cheese,*
> *I lost my poor meatball,*
> *When somebody sneezed.*
> *It rolled off the table,*
> *And onto the floor,*
> *And then my poor meatball,*
> *Rolled out of the door.*
> *It rolled in the garden,*
> *And under a bush,*
> *And then my poor meatball,*
> *Was nothing but mush.*
> *The mush was as tasty,*
> *As tasty could be,*
> *And then the next summer,*

It grew into a tree.
The tree was all covered,
All covered with moss,
And on it grew meatballs,
And tomato sauce.
So if you eat spaghetti,
All covered with cheese,
Hold on to your meatball,
Whenever you sneeze.

God Bless My Underwear

(Sung to "God Bless America")
You can't go wrong with a song about underwear
when camping with kids!

God bless my underwear, my only pair.
Stand beside them and guide them
Through the wash and the wear and the tear.
Through the washer and the dryer
Or the clothesline, back to me,
God bless my underwear, my only pair.
God bless my underwear, my only pair.

I Wish I Were a Little Bar of Soap

(Sung to "If You're Happy and You Know It")

Oh, I wish I were a little bar of soap.
Oh, I wish I were a little bar of soap.
Oh, I'd slippy and I'd slidy over everybody's
   hidey.
Oh, I wish I were a little bar of soap.

Oh, I wish I were a little mos-ki-to.
Oh, I wish I were a little mos-ki-to.
Oh, I'd itchy and I'd bitey under everybody's
   nighty.
Oh, I wish I were a little mos-ki-to.

A Duck May Be Somebody's Mother

(Sung to "Stars and Stripes Forever")

"Be kind to your web-footed friends,
For a duck may be somebody's mother.
Be kind to your friends in the swamp
Where it's very cold and damp. [Rhyme damp
   with swamp.]

You may think that this is the end.
Well it is, but to prove we're all liars,
We're going to sing it again,
Only this time we'll sing a little higher.

[Sing the next verse higher.]

[End with:]
Now you may think that this is the end.
Well it is!

Great Green Gobs of Greasy, Grimy Gopher Guts

(Gross alert! Sung to the tune of "The Old Gray
Mare, She Ain't What She Used to Be")

Great green gobs of greasy, grimy gopher guts
Hurdy gurdey birdie feet
Percolated monkey meat
French fried eyeballs swimmin' in a bowl of
   pus
That's what I had for lunch.
I forgot my spoon!
[Last line is the "Good evening, friends. . . ."–
   style tagline.]

Pink Pajamas

(To the tune of "Battle Hymn of the Republic")

Oh I wear my pink pajamas
In the summer when it's hot.
And I wear my long, white
*   flannels*
In the winter when it's not.
And sometimes in the
*   springtime*
And sometimes in the fall
I JUMP into my sleeping bag
With nothing on at all!
Glory, glory hallelujah.
Glory, glory what's it to ya?
Glory, glory hallelujah.
If I JUMP into my sleeping bag
With nothing on at all!

Add-on Songs

These are great for kids and get their mind off the trail while they think of what animal or machine and sound effect to add.

Once an Austrian Went Yodeling

What interrupts the Austrian's yodeling? You decide in this song, until it all comes down in an avalanche. You get to yodel in this one! The tune is simple. You can find it online or make up one of your own.

Once an Austrian went yodeling on a mountain
*   so high*
When along came a cuckoo bird interrupting
*   his cry.*
Oh lee ah, Oh lee a kee keeah oh lee ah Cuckoo
Oh lee a kee keeah oh lee ah Cuckoo

Oh lee a kee keeah oh lee ah Cuckoo
Oh lee a kee keeah oh.

Once an Austrian went yodeling on a mountain
*   so high*
When along came a grizzly bear interrupting
*   his cry.*
Oh lee ah, Oh lee a kee keeah oh lee ah Cuckoo,
*   Growl!*
Oh lee a kee keeah oh lee ah Cuckoo, Growl!
Oh lee a kee keeah oh lee ah Cuckoo, Growl!
Oh lee a kee keeah oh.

Here are some ideas for other things to come by:
Skier (swish, swish)
Cow (moo, moo)
Duck (quack, quack)
Miss Piggy ("Kermie!")
Girl Scout ("Cookies, Sir?")
Avalanche [This ends the song!]

Alice the Camel

Younger campers love this counting song with a funny ending! Start at 5 or 10. Have campers make up stories about how Alice loses a hump between each verse.

Alice the Camel has 5 humps.
Alice the Camel has 5 humps.
Alice the Camel has 5 humps.
So go Alice, go!

[Decrease the number in each verse.]

Final verse:
Alice the Camel has 1 hump
Alice the Camel has 1 hump
Alice the Camel has 1 hump
So Alice is a horse, of course!

BINGO

It's a classic with clapping replacing each eliminated letter as the song moves along. At the end B-I-N-G-O becomes all claps. Try replacing the word "farmer" with "camper" if you're camping with your pooch!

There was a farmer had a dog,
And Bingo was his name-o.
B-I-N-G-O
B-I-N-G-O
B-I-N-G-O
And Bingo was his name-o.

There was a farmer had a dog,
And Bingo was his name-o.
[clap]-I-N-G-O
[clap]-I-N-G-O
[clap]-I-N-G-O
And Bingo was his name-o.

You Can't Ride in My Little Red Wagon

The sheer volume of this song is really fun. Add your own instructions to get quieter, louder, sing it in funny voices, or whatever you think of.

You can't ride in my little red wagon.
The front wheel's broken and the axel's draggin'.
You can't ride in my little red wagon anymore
    today HA HA HA!!

Second verse same as the first but a whole lot
    louder and a whole lot worse!!
You can't ride in my little red wagon.
The front wheel's broken and the axel draggin'.
You can't ride in my little red wagon anymore
    today HA HA HA !!

Third verse same as the first but a whole lot
    Elmer Fudd and a whole lot worse!
You can't wide in my wittle wed wagon.
The front wheel's woken and the axel waggin'.
You can't wide in my wittle wed wagon any-
    more today [Then laugh like Elmer Fudd.]

Old McDonald

This classic is a great boredom buster on the trail! Get creative with your animals and other funky farm dwellers! Fill in for pig and oink with your creature or object and its noise.

Old McDonald had a farm
E-I-E-I-O
And on that farm he had a pig
E-I-E-I-O
With an oink, oink here
And an oink, oink there
Here an oink
There an oink

Everywhere an oink, oink
Old McDonald had a farm
E-I-E-I-O

Rounds

For the singing family, rounds are the best! It's an easy and kind of magical way to make harmonies. If you don't get it at first, keep trying, concentrate on your part or share it with someone else. You probably know "Row Row Row Your Boat" and "Frère Jacques" and maybe the "Kookaburra" song. Here are a few more great ones. Look them up online if you are not familiar with the tune.

The Canoe Song

My paddle's keen and bright
Flashing with silver
Follow the wild goose flight
Dip, dip and swing
Dip, dip and swing her back
Flashing with silver
Swift as the wild goose flies
Dip, dip and swing

One Bottle of Pop

One bottle of pop, two bottles of pop,
Three bottles of pop, four bottles of pop,
Five bottles of pop, six bottles of pop,
Seven, seven, bottles of pop, pop!

Fish and chips and vinegar, vinegar, vinegar
Fish and chips and vinegar,
Pepper, pepper, pepper, salt!

Photo by David Rolf

Don't throw your trash in my backyard,
My backyard, my backyard.
Don't throw your trash in my backyard,
My backyard's full!

Hey Ho

(Sung in a minor key, this one can be really pretty. Similar rounds are "Ah, Poor Bird" and "Rose, Rose")

Hey, ho, nobody home
No meat nor drink
Nor money have I none
Still I will be very merry
Hey, ho, nobody home

Classic Campfire and Folk Songs

There are so many fun traditional campfire songs! Consider purchasing a songbook or look online at Boy Scout and Girl Scout websites for a fairly comprehensive list.

"The Ants Go Marching"

"When the Saints Go Marching In"

"Yankee Doodle Dandy"

Here are a couple classics:

Photo by David Rolf

Sipping Cider through a Straw

The first part of every verse is Repeat-after-Me style. If someone has a guitar, the chords are included.

/ G - / / D - / G - / - - C - / D - G - /

The prettiest girl (the prettiest girl)
I ever saw (I ever saw)
Was sippin' ci- (was sippin' ci-)
Der through a straw (der through a straw)
The prettiest girl I ever saw
Was sippin' cider through a straw

I said to her, "What ya doin' that fer"
A sippin' ci-der through a straw . . .

First cheek to cheek, then jaw to jaw
We both sipped cider through a straw . . .

Here is a partial list to get you going:

"A Bear Went Over the Mountain"

"Frog Went A-Courting"

"Baby Bumblebee"

"There Was a Desperado"

"Drunken Sailor"

"Down Down Baby"

"Cat Came Back"

"Camptown Races"

"Blow the Man Down"

"Billy Boy"

"He's Got the Whole World"

"I've Been Working on the Railroad"

John Jacob Jingle Heimer Schmitt

John Jacob Jingle Heimer Schmitt,
That's my name too . . .
Whenever I go out,
People always shout . . .
"John Jacob Jingle Heimer Schmitt,"
Da, da, da, da, da, da!
Repeat four times, each time softer, until on the
    last verse no sound comes out except:
Da, da, da, da, da, da!

Photo by David Rolf

Every now and then, that straw would slip
And we'd sip ci-der lip to lip . . .

That's how I got my mother-in-law
By sippin' ci-der through a straw . . .

Now forty-nine kids, all call me Pa
From sippin' ci-der through a straw . . .

The moral of this sad, sad, joke
Is don't sip ci-der, sip a Coke!

CHAPTER 9

CONTINUING THE FUN BACK HOME

Coming home after camping in the outdoors, there are a few things you can do immediately to keep the family togetherness going and continue with the fun.

You have been working together and playing together for a weekend or longer. Set expectations that everyone will help unload the car and unpack when you get home. Then, encourage showers and baths and watch the dirt flow off. It'll feel great.

Whether you're eating on the road or at home with takeout or leftovers, try to have a family dinner your first night back. Ask each person to reflect on the camping experience. Ask them what they saw and did, their favorite moments and activities, tough moments, something new they learned. At bedtime, perhaps your child's book can be her NATURE JOURNAL.

Encourage your children to keep using their NATURE JOURNALS at home. There's a lot of critters and plant life even in backyards and parks.

Look up the answers to all the questions you logged while observing nature. Add them to your NATURE JOURNAL.

> *What do parents owe their young that is more important than a warm and trusting connection to the Earth . . .?*
>
> —Theodore Roszak,
> *The Voice of the Earth*

Do the "Back At Home" follow-ups to any of the activities in this book that had them.

couldn't identify on the trail. Take in a sunset.

Keep playing games together. Consider creating a weekly Games Night for the family. Keep the Family Conversation Starters going at the dinner table, in the car, and at other times the family is together. Now that you have created some new family traditions, perhaps you can make room for them in the daily rigmarole. Even faced with the same old daily routines, the fun doesn't have to end!

Get out in nature often with your family. And start planning your next camping trip!

It's time to do something with all the pictures taken. Consider printing some and pasting them in the NATURE JOURNAL or making a photo book or slideshow to share with the family. Try to do this right away, while you still have momentum.

Plan a family adventure day trip, biking, fishing, or hiking somewhere near home. Look for geocaches in your area. Check out guides in your public library to look up the animals and plants you

THE JEWELS IN A GEODE

Cracking open geodes is one way to continue your study of geology and the magic of nature at home. You can buy geodes—rocks in which crystals grow—at any rock shop or online.

ACTIVITY FINDER

Quiet Time Games

These are games that are good for early in the morning or late at night or any time that some rest or relaxation is needed.

Energy Busters

These are games for getting the fidgets out!

Recommended for Preteens and Teens (11 to 18)

All of the activities in this book are appropriate for tweens and teens, but the following are especially good for these older kids who may benefit from time off from their phones and social media.

Solo Activities

Activities that one person/child can do alone without extra supervision or adult guidance.

ACKNOWLEDGMENTS

A big thank-you to all the families that helped beta test activities in the book on camping trips and in parks and those who served as models for photographs. My appreciation goes out to all the photographers who contributed images to this book, and a loud shout out to the talented David Rolf and photographer extraordinaire Kevin Meynell (kevinmeynell.com).

Thank you to Doug Cantwell, supervisor at Lake Temescal, and East Bay Regional Park District, for letting us take pictures in that beautiful setting.

Thanks to Katie Benoit Cardoso at Globe Pequot for giving me the chance to write this book and to Imee Curiel for all her wonderful editing advice that helped to shape the final book.

I want to recognize Traver Huggins, Alex Krichevsky, and other family members and friends for their contributions of favorite outdoor activities and games. Thanks to Nelly's Java for a table to work on and great coffee, as well as OakStop. Thanks to Mom and Dad for taking us to Silver Lake every summer. A special thank you to my sons, Ben and Max, who gave me feedback on games and ideas for activities and did just about all the fun stuff in this book. Major gratitude goes to my husband, Doug, for his support, belief, and love.

ABOUT THE AUTHOR

Linda Parker Hamilton is the author of the Falcon Guides *Best Hikes Near San Francisco, Hiking the San Francisco Bay,* and *Camping Northern California*. She has written, edited, and published over twenty exciting histories, biographies, memoirs, and family histories for her business Stories to Last, including *Chasing Spring* about resilience, beauty, and escape from Nazi Germany. She has also written numerous stories for magazines, newspapers, and websites, including *American Heritage of Science & Technology,* the *San Francisco Chronicle, California Magazine,* and the Library of Congress's site for children and families: AmericasStory.gov. Prior to all this she worked in the travel-tech industry and taught public school for ten years. Linda is also a singer-songwriter. She lives with her husband and two sons, Ben and Max, in Oakland, California.